SELF-DIRECTED LEARNING GUIDE

STUDY WHIZ™

SECOND EDITION

Clif St. Germain

Deb Fetch

Gene Brewer

Published by The Center For Academic Excellence
608 Lafitte Street
Mandeville, LA 70448
1.888.455.LEARN

www.studywhiz.com

Copyright © 2009 Clif J. St. Germain.
StudyWhiz United States trademark registration number 2485004.

All rights reserved. When forms and sample documents are included, their use is authorized only by educators, local school sites, and/or noncommercial or nonprofit entities that have purchased the book. Except for that usage and as permitted under Sections 107 or 108 of the 1976 United States Copyright Act, no part of this book may be reproduced or utilized in any form or by any means, electronic or mechanical, including photocopying, recording, or by any information storage and retrieval system, without permission in writing from the publisher.

The Blackline Masters are contained within a CD available for purchase separate from this publication. These masters may be reprinted for limited classroom use without prior permission so long as they are reprinted for students who own a copy of the StudyWhiz™ and copyright notice appears on each copy.

ISBN 978-0-615-25970-3

Authors:
Clif St. Germain, Ph.D.
Deb Fetch, M.Ed.
Gene Brewer, Ed.D.

Creator, Mitosis MindFrames:
Gabrielle St. Germain

Design:
Licci Zemleduch
sevensiete@mac.com

Cover Image Credit:
Aldo Murillo

Editor:
Michelle Nash

Proofreader:
Nancy Picard

Pages 39-41 from THE AMERICAN NATION 2005 SURVEY STUDENT EDITION by Davidson and Stoff. © Copyright 2005 Pearson Education, Inc. or its affiliate(s). Used by permission. All Rights Reserved.

DEDICATION

This book is dedicated to all students who want to learn without strife, much from many, being taught by all... and ...

To my children, Gabrielle and Brad, who have taught me much about learning and life.
- Clif

To my mother, Elaine Beyer, for always encouraging me to trust and follow my heart ... I know you're watching, smiling, and sending waves of unending love from above.
- Deb

To the memory of Dr. Anne Woods Bell for stimulating my interest in the brain and its relevance to education. While she rests from her labors, her good works continue to live and bless students with the concepts of brain compatible education.
- Gene

CONTENTS

Section I

An Open Letter to Students 2

How StudyWhiz Will Help You Succeed In School 4

Note to Parents and Teachers...................................... 6

Introduction: A Defining Moment 10

Section II

Previewing 32

Naming 48

Connecting 78

Recapping 98

Constructing 107

Self-Testing 117

Reflecting 124

Section III

StudyWhiz Taxonomy 138

Project Guide 141

SECTION 1

An Open Letter to Students

How StudyWhiz Will Help You Succeed In School

Note to Parents and Teachers

Introduction: A Defining Moment

From: Clif St. Germain, Deb Fetch, Gene Brewer
Subject: This is *your* lucky day!
To: You!

Dear Student,

This is *your* lucky day!

If you're holding this book, then you're still in school. And I bet there are times when you'd like to do better, improve your grades, finish your homework, and still have time left to spare!

We, at StudyWhiz, want you to know: All those things *are* possible. You'll see.

It's sad that many people confuse being smart with having a high I.Q. (Intelligence Quotient). The truth is, being *intelligent* is not at all the same as being *smart*.

Intelligence describes a property of the mind that involves many related capabilities, such as the ability to reason, solve problems, think abstractly, use language, and understand ideas. Some experts teach that intelligence also includes creativity, emotions, and personality.

> Do you have a friend you would describe as highly intelligent? Several names are probably popping into your head. Do all of them get straight A's?

Smart, on the other hand, describes the ability to effectively gather facts, practice in ways that improve performance, and form conclusions to help you achieve a desired goal.

Smart is more about using your brain to *your* advantage than about using your brain to reason. In other words, *being smart* is **what you do with what you have.**

As such, being smart is something everybody can get better at. The StudyWhiz motto is this: "Smart Is Self Taught." We hope you agree!

Most people are smarter than they know. Your brain is a sneaky little organ that quietly nudges you in the right direction without giving you a clue. Scientists tell us that 90% of our thinking goes on slightly below our level of consciousness, which means you're thinking without knowing it. It's harder to stop than to start!

The secret to becoming smarter is to learn *how* you are naturally smart—and develop these talents to your advantage. For the more you understand how your brain learns and can direct this incredible guidance system, the more your school performance will improve. There is only one catch. Getting smarter takes practice. It is a trial and error process that

requires . . . work. You will need to be on a best-friend basis with your incredible pattern-making brain and practice using it on purpose.

That's why smartness can only be self-taught.

Then you can practice **thinking** about your own **thinking**. This is mental work that can be learned. (Eating brain-food and getting brain-rest is part of the work!)

==If your goal is to enjoy school, get awesome grades and prepare for future success, decide now to become a self-directed and life-long learner.==

Repeat after me: I WILL (*I will*) BECOME A (*become a*) SELF-DIRECTED (*self-directed*) AND LIFE-LONG (*and life-long*) LEARNER! (**LEARNER!**).

You must also learn to create a good fit between how your brain works best and what you are trying to accomplish. In school, this means discovering how you can overcome personal challenges. StudyWhiz will help with that too.

StudyWhiz helps you teach yourself to learn in smarter ways. That's why it's called "self-directed." If you are making average grades, you can expect those grades to improve. If you are already making above average grades, expect exceptional grades. If you are struggling in school (or in one subject area), brace yourself for the shock of your life.

We told you this would be your lucky day!

Respectively,

Clif St. Germain
Deb Fetch
Gene Brewer

What is the difference between "intelligent" and "smart"?

Think of someone you know who is very smart. What characteristics lead you to believe that he/she is smart? List them and share with your teacher and your classmates.

1. _____
2. _____
3. _____
4. _____
5. _____

Someone is probably writing your name on their list. (If they aren't, they should!)

How StudyWhiz Will Help You Succeed in School

SMILE! I'm going to take a picture of your face.

Now, *CLAP!* While I snap a picture of your hands.

Okay, now *THINK!* Hey, I just took a picture of your brain!

Don't believe me? Okay, I'll admit it. I lied on the last one. But I'm not lying about this: I can teach you how to create your own photograph of your brain thinking.

Stay with me here. StudyWhiz's new way of learning helps you actually **see** your thoughts. Not only that, but with StudyWhiz you can also add color, form, and order to your thoughts to help you remember what you've learned.

> StudyWhiz is a secret learning system that helps students to organize their thoughts in their brains. And it's no secret that your brain is key to success in school.

Learning is natural. You (and everyone else) have been thinking and learning since the day you were born. But most students have no idea *how* they learn. Fewer yet know how to think!

The first simple step to success in school is this: **Understand how you think and how you learn.** Repeat that rule three times. (See, aren't you feeling smarter already?)

Try this: What are you thinking about right now? Can you **see** your thoughts? Could you explain what is going on in your head in a way that would make sense to someone else?

It's like dot-to-dot: Your brain connects thoughts to create ideas. If you have a problem picturing your thoughts, don't worry. Most people can't. That's why you need Study-Whiz.

With StudyWhiz, you will practice thinking out loud. Students who excel in school are somehow more aware of their thinking. They actually practice thinking—much as one would practice basketball or trumpet.

But first you have to understand what thinking is all about. The more you practice thinking--which leads to learning—the easier and more fun school will be.

Once you **see** your ideas, you can then arrange them. And once you arrange them, you can learn them. And once you learn them, you can remember them. And there's nothing better than that!

Think about what you just read. Now, create a slogan or catchy rhyme that describes the importance of making your thoughts visible. Use symbols and colors to make your work more interesting. Remember, your task is to capture the main ideas you just read in a way that is interesting as well as accurate. Share your work with your classmates.

Making Thinking Visible

Practice doesn't make perfect, but practice does make permanent. Take advantage of your brain—and become a whiz by learning how to organize your thoughts. You're already smart. StudyWhiz will help you become smarter.

And when you get your next report card, don't forget to comb your hair and put on your favorite shirt. Then stand by the wall and . . . SMILE.

Someone special might want to take your picture!

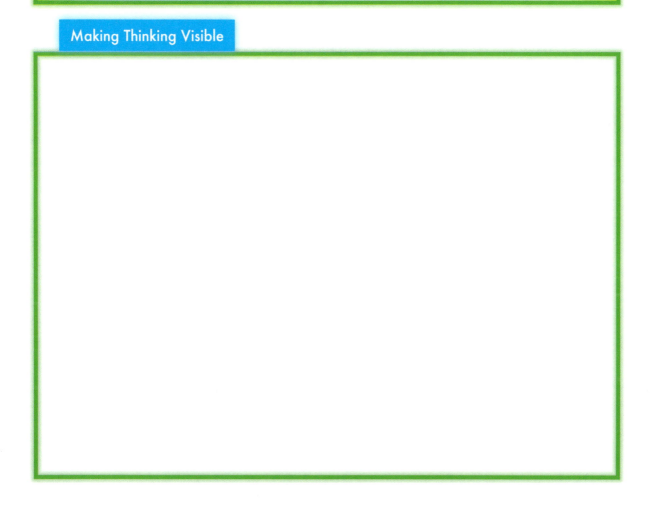

Note to Parents and Teachers

In 1987 Clif St. Germain developed StudyWhiz for use in his Learning Center in Mandeville, Louisiana. In 2000, he converted StudyWhiz to a self-study learning guide, trademarked and distributed for teachers to use with students. As a result, thousands of students have enriched the quality of their school experience and improved their academic performance.

In 2008 Dr. St. Germain, along with educators Deb Fetch and Dr. Gene Brewer, revised and updated StudyWhiz to incorporate advances in the science of learning.

However, the central message of StudyWhiz's initial vision has not changed: **"Smart is Self-Taught."**

> Success in school is strongly linked to the learner's ability to convert what is being taught into content that *makes sense*. StudyWhiz does exactly that: It provides a framework for learning that enhances understanding.

Students need to learn how to study smart! In StudyWhiz, students make their thinking visible. That is, they **leave tracks of their thinking** that can be used effectively in testing and homework. StudyWhiz's goal is for students to take control of their own learning. Learners are changed from passive, teacher-dependent students to active, confident, self-directed students.

The following will answer common questions from teachers and parents:

What are the benefits of teaching students to become more self-directed?

Self-directed students are more active, confident, independent and purposeful learners. However, a learner cannot be self-directed without working out a learning system that best suits his or her own temperament and skills set. Again, no one can hand a learner a self-directed learning system: The learner must develop and perfect these skills over time.

Students don't come to school with self-directed learning skills. Most students begin school excited about learning, but, over time, formal "traditional" classrooms become an advantage only to students who learn best in that environment. Those students are then labeled "smart."

For the thousands of students who don't fit traditional teaching methods, learning can become tedious and unfulfilling.

For a non-traditional learner to succeed in school, he or she must work out a personalized learning system. Self-directed learners discover that teaching will only take them so far. After that, they are on their own.

In a sense, self-directed learners have learned that "smart" is a subject they must teach themselves. This is where StudyWhiz comes in. **StudyWhiz is a visual framework that sets in motion the development of personal and adaptive learning tools.** These tools will work in any classroom, any school, at most any level.

StudyWhiz requires students to *think about their thinking* in systematic ways. At the same time it gives "wiggle room" to modify and personalize the study system.

If we have discovered anything about learning in the last two decades, it is that one size does not fit all. A study system guided by how the brain learns just makes good sense. This is exactly what StudyWhiz does.

Why don't teachers teach students to become self-directed learners?

Good question. Truthfully, teaching students to learn in systematic ways is not difficult. In fact, students love to think and talk about what they are learning. They also love to interact as they learn.

But teachers are asked to accomplish and cover so much that they don't have time to teach students how to learn. Some parents model these behaviors at home, and some students grasp it intuitively. But most students have no concept how to learn systematically. In other words, they *do not know* how to study!

How does StudyWhiz help students make better sense of their schoolwork?

Most inefficient learners are seriously weak in organization skills. They waste energy spinning their wheels—and getting nowhere!

StudyWhiz provides a step-by-step progression of learning prompts that helps students become more efficient by emphasizing how ideas fit together.

How do these learning prompts work?

StudyWhiz is organized into seven interrelated skills. Specific "prompts" draw attention to the brain's capacity to make sense of the world. These thinking prompts are called "Mind-Frames" because each represents learning from a slightly different perspective—just as changing picture frames can transform a painting's effect.

Combined, these seven MindFrames follow the natural cycle of all learning. Think about learning in this progression:

- **Preview:** Set the stage for learning
- **Name:** Draw attention to important differences
- **Connect:** Group information for ease of learning and memorizing
- **Recap:** Self-monitor learning progress

- **Construct:** Use it or lose it
- **Self-test:** Provide evidence of learning
- **Reflect:** Take perspective and make learning personal

How is StudyWhiz being used?

- As a study guide for parents helping students at home
- By individual students for improving their performance in schools
- As a support text for learning in regular classrooms
- In home schooling programs
- As a guide for Big Brother, Big Sister activities
- As a supplemental text for Title 1 programs
- As a text for summer transition to high school programs
- In vocational education programs
- As a text for study skills courses
- In ninth grade academy programs
- In mentoring programs
- By learning and tutorial centers

What results can be expected from using StudyWhiz?

- Improved grades and performance on tests
- Increased levels of confidence and self-directed learning
- More efficient use of study time
- Enhanced ability to think about learning in purposeful ways
- Higher levels of organization in note taking, problem solving, applying, synthesizing, and summarizing learning
- Increased confidence for meeting learning challenges and taking active control and responsibility for learning
- MOST IMPORTANTLY, students come to think of learning as natural, fun, and rewarding. *Because it is!*

A whiz is a person with a remarkable skill. For example, you've heard someone called a "computer whiz" or a "trivia whiz."

Imagine every student in school becoming a study whiz!

StudyWhiz believes that is possible. *How* students study matters as much as *what* they study. Students will quickly catch on that "Smart is Self-Taught." Then they will figure out that being self-directed is **smart**. And after that, academic success is not only possible—it's probable!

StudyWhiz's vision and hope are that students *whiz* to the top of the class, gain confidence, and jump-start their journey towards becoming lifelong learners!

Introduction: A Defining Moment

 ### Imagine life without cell phones!

No text messaging, no leaving voice messages, and no freedom to talk wherever and whenever you want.

Today, most teens would not consider leaving home without their cell phone! (Do you think it's possible to be addicted to a cell phone?)

If you have your own cell phone but didn't pick it out yourself, you probably at least made sure your parents knew exactly which one you wanted. But there's so many to choose from!

This may shock you, but selecting a cell phone and succeeding in school involve the **same** thinking skills.

StudyWhiz calls these thinking skills **MindFrames.**

Think: **Mind + Frame**. A frame holds a picture or a poster. In a similar way, your mind should hold a picture of what to do next when studying. Your mind is the frame; the pictures are the seven steps. (Hang in there—you'll catch on soon.)

Take a look at the following seven steps. Each step is a **MindFrame.** Together we will explore how choosing the perfect cell phone involves the same kind of thinking as studying for a science test.

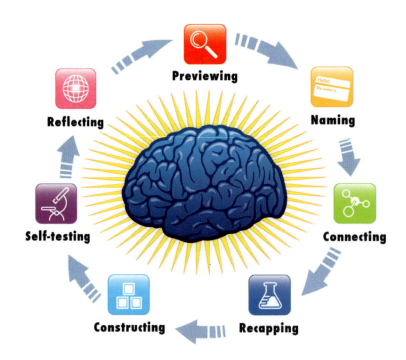

Step 1: Previewing

When it comes to cell phones, teens want them usually for different reasons than adults. Teens use their phones for more than just talking: they text-message, instant-message, and multimedia-message. Plus, they use their cell for music. (Can you think of other ways teens use cell phones?)

With an Internet-capable phone, teens can also network on websites. But as much as teens love all the latest gizmos and gadgets, adding on those things also adds on to the cost.

So, you would need to compare different cell phone and networking companies to find the perfect phone—within your budget. But how would you begin?

First, you would probably start noticing ads and commercials. Cell phone companies know that—and they want your business. So be smart—and do your homework!

You probably will also notice your friends' phones and ask about the different features. Then you might search the Internet, download brochures, and maybe even visit cell phone stores.

All of this is called **previewing**. You PREVIEW the information to get a feel for the highlights of each phone and the various payment plans. Previewing gives you a better sense of what to do next. It's the jump-start towards making a wise purchase.

Let's review again the important steps you would have taken in the previewing process.

Previewing

- You looked through numerous web sites and brochures focusing on words and details that stood out.
- You skimmed.
- You scanned.
- You skipped what was not important to your decision.
- You noticed what you liked or disliked about each phone.
- You asked friends about their phones' features.

This shows how your mind PREVIEWS new ideas. It's smart shopping—but that's not all.

Previewing should also happen in school when you are about to face new material. By thumbing through an upcoming chapter, your mind is creating an overall impression. It's getting a "jump start" on the next lesson.

For example, you just took an earth science chapter test. Chapter Six is next. As you look through (preview) the upcoming pages, you might be thinking: "Good, I already know most of this," or "Oh dear, this looks hard," or "Hmmm, interesting," or "Maybe I can bribe the teacher to skip this chapter." (Good luck with that one!)

As in your initial planning for a new cell phone, **previewing** gives you clues as to what's coming—before turning to the details.

Actually, **previewing** doesn't take long, but it does give you a head start on the material, and it will increase your chances for getting a good grade on the chapter test. Knowing that, who would ever think to skip the PREVIEW process? Not one successful student!

Do you know that 80 percent of what you need to learn is found in 20 percent of what you study? (More statistics from research.) This is known as the 80/20 Rule. No wonder it's a time-saver to know *what you're going to study even before you begin.*

Previewing also eliminates the mystery of what is going to be important, because already you're checking out the bold words, italics, colored type, vocabulary box, pictures with captions—and sometimes even the questions at the end (briefly). Remember: Don't look for details. Just skim for the "big picture."

(Hint: Teachers should help you with this, but if they forget—or don't know how! —then do it yourself. Hey, maybe *you* can teach the teacher!)

Previewing also highlights interesting information while it relaxes you about content you have already learned. *Whew—I studied that last year, so this section will be a breeze.*

And, it gives you an insight into how the whole chapter is organized. *Let's see, first we'll study this (which I know), then that (which I don't know), then some vocab, then a review, then some practice problems, then we're done. I can do this!*

If you think of previewing as the **warm-up stage,** you'll know why it's important. Can you imagine an athlete competing without first warming up? Never! Can you imagine a singer or a pianist performing without warming up? No! Can you imagine tackling new information without previewing it first? Of course not!

Without previewing, self-directed learning is impossible. But by surveying the chapter and generating a few insights and questions, you will improve your concentration, memory, and learning.

Call this the 100/100 rule: 100 percent guaranteed . . . 100 percent of the time.

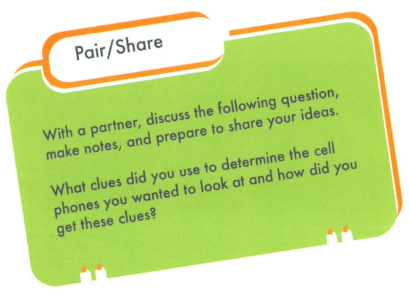

Pair/Share

With a partner, discuss the following question, make notes, and prepare to share your ideas.

What clues did you use to determine the cell phones you wanted to look at and how did you get these clues?

Picture yourself out of the gate and down the road to success.

Now you're ready for Step 2—which involves taking a closer look at the material. If you've previewed well, you'll be more than ready to dive into the details!

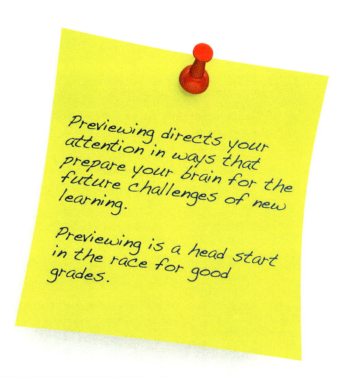

Previewing directs your attention in ways that prepare your brain for the future challenges of new learning.

Previewing is a head start in the race for good grades.

Step 2: Naming

After **previewing** many cell phones and cell phone plans, it's time to shift your attention to NAMING—out loud or on paper—the similarities and differences between each.

Be aware that benefits (the exciting, enticing options) are often in LARGE print, while the drawbacks (what is and is not included in the price) are in small print. If you own a magnifying glass, you might want to grab it!

With an ever-growing market for the sale of cell phone services to teens, the various cell phone providers have a wide variety of choices to meet your needs. Here are some popular names for these plans—and more will surely be coming:

Stand-Alone Plan. (Your own cell phone account and bill, limited minutes, with a per-minute cost after those minutes are used up.)

Companion Plan. (Phone added to parent's account, minutes shared among multiple phones. These plans often include unlimited minutes for phones on same plan.)

Local Unlimited Plan. (Unlimited minutes for local and incoming calls, charges per minute for long distance calls.)

Prepaid Plan. (Phone minutes prepaid. When gone, so is the cell service.)

So, with these choices in mind, you set out to NAME the plans, along with their benefits and drawbacks:

- Does it offer free or unlimited text messaging?
- How many minutes can you talk and for what price?
- Does it include free mobile to mobile?
- Are there free nights and weekend calling?
- Does it have calling circles with unlimited free calling?
- Does it include rollover minutes?
- What about roaming charges?
- Does it include a free cell phone option?
- What features and downloads are available?
- Do they have picture and video messaging?
- Can you download music and ringtones?

You are asking yourself questions, seeking answers, and looking for the differences in the individual carriers. This NAMES important information so you can retrieve it when it's time to make an informed decision. Suggestion: Take good notes on what you learn. (Then sell them to your friends later—and upgrade your phone!)

Remember that NAMING involves details. If **PREVIEWING** is the forest, then **NAMING** is the trees.

Naming

- You jotted down the names of special features for each type of cell phone.
- On your notes you may have highlighted favorite sections in the brochure.
- You put your ideas in your own words because they will mean more to you.
- You paid special attention to the names of the special features so that you could ask good questions.

That's how your mind NAMES new material when learning. A name conveys that something is different from something else. It tells you to pay attention for a special reason. Names help you organize your thoughts. And names help you remember.

Okay, back to schoolwork. Once you have previewed a chapter, you now want to shift your attention to the details, supporting facts, important people, events, and ideas. To do this you will NAME what you want to know in ways that make sense to you.

Without names, it would be difficult to distinguish between people and things. A name is a valuable label. Think about it: A cell phone and an iPod—two devices that are different but similar in that most teens are never far from either!

Their differences allow you to name them and talk about them intelligently—their functions, their features, and their costs. What if you didn't have names for these devices?

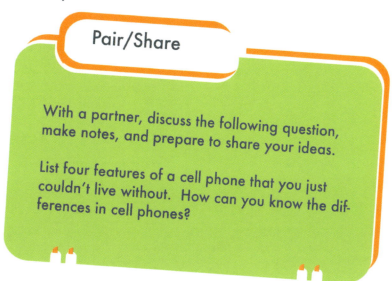

Pair/Share

With a partner, discuss the following question, make notes, and prepare to share your ideas.

List four features of a cell phone that you just couldn't live without. How can you know the differences in cell phones?

> Names are critical to the learning process. Names alone retrieve information from your memory—whether objects, events, or textbook concepts.

When taking notes from a book or a teacher, you are recording the names of important ideas in ways that help you study and remember them.

So you preview the big picture, then you focus in on the details, which at this point are the names. Soon you'll be ready to extend the learning by making connections.

Meanwhile, you're getting closer and closer to purchasing that cell phone—and succeeding in school.

Step 3 CONNECTING is about considering possibilities—*possibly* the most fun framework yet.

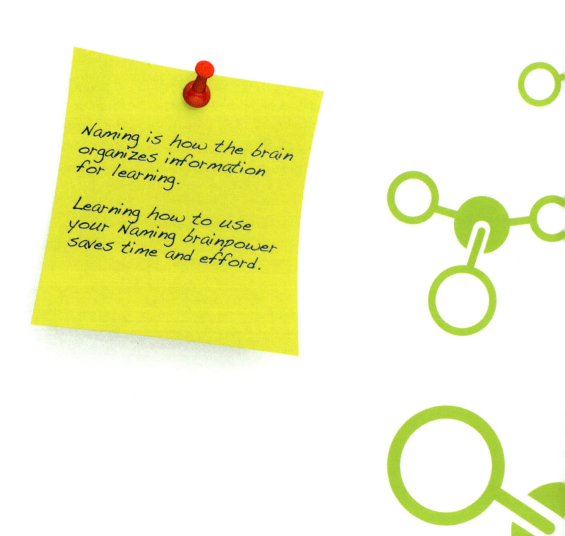

Naming is how the brain organizes information for learning.

Learning how to use your Naming brainpower saves time and effort.

Step 3: Connecting

You've **named** each cell phone company's plan—and one or two appeal to you more than the others.

Now it's time to CONNECT the information by comparing rate plans from all carriers based on the features most important to you. Organizing the options side by side will probably help. Then, on your notes, highlight what you like from the following:

- Basic monthly charges
- Anytime minutes
- Free night and weekend minutes
- Per minute airtime rates for exceeded minutes
- Roaming charges
- Hours per day for peak versus off-peak minutes
- Charges for text messages
- Different phone options
- Features and downloads, picture and video messaging, games, music, etc.

Connecting

To connect, you asked yourself:

→ "Could I use this cell phone to keep up with the social scene?"
→ "Could I use this cell phone to text friends about the answers to homework assignments?"
→ "Does this cell phone video capture and allow me to pick my own ringtones and personalize the screen saver?"
→ "Could I call my parents to inform them about my whereabouts and plans?"
→ "Will I be able to link into the school web site to check my grades and assignments?"

What great questions! And that's exactly how your mind CONNECTS when learning in school.

It tells you how the different parts fit together in ways that make sense. CONNECTING invites the mind to search for meaningful ways to organize things.

> Successfully **naming** what you are learning lays the foundation for making **connections** of all kinds. **Connecting ideas increases your ability to remember what you are learning.**

See, your brain stores information by *similarity*. Connections illustrate these similarities in ways that are more easily recalled. And recalling is what brings back the right answers on tests! Connecting is really an important bridge to understanding.

Building thinking maps is an excellent way for you to make connections. Thinking maps are visual representations of how ideas contained in a chapter are related. Names are usually limited to words. But, thinking maps allow your spatial intelligence to shine because they include pictures, shapes, patterns, symbols, doodles, colors, and logo graphics.

Thinking maps make your thoughts visible so you can conceptualize what you are learning in more complete ways. Thinking maps also promote discussion and help you explore specific topics in creative and organized ways. You can use them as road maps to deeper understanding. One thing is for certain: connecting ideas by creating thinking maps is a powerful memory jogger.

Pair/Share

With a partner, discuss the following question, make notes, and prepare to share your ideas.

Why is a picture worth a thousand words? Hint: Patterns that make sense get the brain's attention.

A picture truly *is* worth a thousand words. (Besides, most teens enjoy doodling.) Trust me, the hard part's over. Step 4 RECAPPING means basically checking for comprehension. Are you ready to buy now, or is there still more you need to know?

Hopefully not—but this is why the RECAP step is so (very-very!) important.

Connecting builds memory power. It is another way that "Smart" is self-taught.

Step 4: Recapping

You have the cell phone information plotted in your mind or on paper.

But are you absolutely sure you're ready to make an informed decision—with no regrets? Maybe there's more information about a carrier's plan—or phone features—that you forgot to ask.

RECAPPING is deciding if you've asked all the right questions and if you've understood all the answers.

Recapping

- ☑ Have I examined each brochure completely and fairly?
- ☑ Have I considered all the features I need?
- ☑ Have I compared costs?
- ☑ Have I examined the fine print and the rate plan?
- ☑ Do I have enough information to make a good decision?

That's exactly how your mind RECAPS when learning. It goes back to the beginning and looks over every item one more time before moving forward.

The connections you have made need to stand up to scrutiny—yours! They need to be challenged for accuracy. Before becoming a self-directed learner, you may have regarded that as something your teacher did. But no longer.

That's why once the previewing, naming, and connecting steps are completed, it's time to self-check. RECAPPING is that point in the learning cycle when your brain backtracks and asks, "How well am I doing? Do I know this information well enough to move on to new learning?"

After all, the more skilled you are at monitoring your own learning, the more prepared you will be to learn new information in the future.

Recapping is like a midway check, where you can honestly say, "Yes, I am learning here. I get it!"

Recapping is an opportunity to give yourself a well-deserved pat on the back. (Go ahead and do that right now. You deserve it.)

It is also a timely reminder that you may have to go back and re-learn something you missed along the way. The better you become at monitoring your own progress, the more self-directed your learning will become.

> The central message of step #4 ("RECAPPING") is this: Before moving forward, stop and check your progress.

Students who either don't understand the importance of recapping or don't take the time to monitor their progress, run the risk of becoming overwhelmed. The next danger is that they will lose their way—and give up.

Imagine going to all the work of previewing and naming and connecting—and then decide not to buy the cell phone after all. Are you serious?

In school, you don't want to preview a chapter and name the important points and then make connections—all in preparation for getting a good grade—and then give up before asking: Is there any part of this I didn't understand or learn well?

Recapping is not only important—it's exciting. When smart kids RECAP, they do it energetically! *Really?* Absolutely!

Now you're ready to demonstrate that you know enough to make a good cell phone purchase. You have surveyed the available options and narrowed your choices. You named important differences in features and cost. You looked for patterns and made sure you touched all the bases.

On to Step 5 CONSTRUCTING, which is where the action is!

Pair/Share

With a partner, discuss the following question, make notes, and prepare to share your ideas.

What are some reasons why people purchase a cell phone that they later realize isn't right for them?

Recapping is all about knowing what you know.

It is also about making what's important a high priority.

Step 5: Constructing

Are you excited about finally selecting your new cell phone? Sure you are. You've done the research. You're smart about every aspect of cell phones. And you *will* make the right decision regarding three key areas:

- **Rate Plan**. Am I spending as little as possible each month to get what I need from my service?
- **Coverage**. Does the phone work where and when I need it?
- **Cell Phone Features.** Does the phone do what I want? Is it within my budget, or my parent's budget, and am I getting the best possible deal?

CONSTRUCTING involves hands-on experimenting, trying out, and acting on the research!

Constructing

- Can I try out different models in the store?
- Can I bring another cell phone to compare features while I test the phone in the store?
- Can I test to see how well the cell phone video captures and how well it downloads music?

Finally your hands are on your brand new cell phone. You're dialing. You're talking and listening and texting and . . . well, whatever you've been wanting a cell phone for. Now you're doing it—finally!

And that's exactly what happens when your mind CONSTRUCTS new learning. It uses the learning to achieve a further goal.

Constructing is the "use it or lose it" step in the learning process. Here learning shifts from listening, organizing ideas, thinking, reflecting, and monitoring to demonstrating mastery. You didn't research cell phones for the fun of it. You researched so you could get the best cell phone and use it.

In school, you don't learn to forget it all later. You learn to remember— and use the information. (Do teachers bother to tell students they are supposed to use this stuff?) Understanding doesn't just happen. Simply being exposed to information is not enough.

> Constructing involves making use of what you have learned in ways that demonstrate understanding. The CONSTRUCTING Step is where the action is. No wonder students love this part the most!

You are constructing when you figure out the answers to end-of-chapter questions, when you give a presentation, when you suggest a solution to a problem, when you prepare a science project or experiment, when you edit or write a paper, when you work in a group to complete an assignment, when you write a poem, when you defend your opinion, when you evaluate alternative points of view, or when you use technology for research.

Teachers often call constructing "guided practice." Or homework! (Just kidding). Constructing also involves creating study materials that summarize what you have learned in preparation for a unit test.

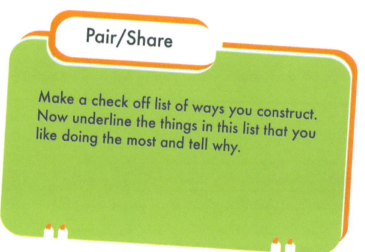

Pair/Share

Make a check off list of ways you construct. Now underline the things in this list that you like doing the most and tell why.

When a student can say, "I not only learned these facts, I know how to use them in my life," his or her mind is in the CONSTRUCTING stage.

And that is something to celebrate! (Like maybe you'll want to construct a cake—and have your own party? Don't forget to call all your friends—on your new cell phone!)

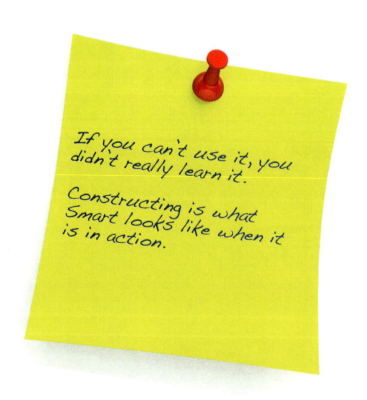

If you can't use it, you didn't really learn it.

Constructing is what smart looks like when it is in action.

Step 6: Self-Testing

Hopefully your new cell phone will work when you need it and how you need it.

The good news is that all national carriers now subscribe to the wireless industry's consumer code. This code provides that new customers will get at least a 14-day trial period to try out a carrier's service, with no penalty if the service is canceled. That means, if your new phone doesn't meet your expectations, you will be charged for any used airtime, but you can cancel the plan and return the phone with no early termination fees during that trial period.

Self-Testing

Can I take the phone home for a 14-day trial period to test it in "real time?"

That's exactly what your mind does when it SELF-TESTS new learning. It gives you a warm-up (a practice) for whatever test awaits you.

Self-testing helps get rid of pre-test fears—really!

Each of the Learning Steps included in the StudyWhiz process will help you build confidence and reduce anxiety during testing. During the SELF-TEST phase, you should test yourself often so that exams and final tests will not seem as threatening.

Use your notes and thinking maps, and review your practice assignments. By writing sample test questions and creating study cards, you will improve your performance. A major component of the Self-Testing Step is to summarize what you have learned in ways that might be on a final exam: essays, fill in the blank, vocabulary, matching, etc.

Another recommended part of self-testing is to study with a classmate. Your friend will point out what you still don't know. (And you'll do the same back.)

Self-directed learners consider tests to be part of the learning process. They also see mistakes as opportunities for learning.

> The central message of the Self-Testing Step is to actively prepare yourself for a test and to avoid discouragement if the results are not what you expected.

Every person that ever lived knows what it's like to take a test and feel like you knew more than your grade shows. Or that you studied all the wrong things.

But if you've gone through the preview, name, connect, recap, construct, and self-test steps, *you have learned* in ways that make remembering and understanding more likely. And isn't that what matters most anyway?

There's always next time to get that A!

Pair/Share

With a partner, write a test question about one of the learning steps described here.

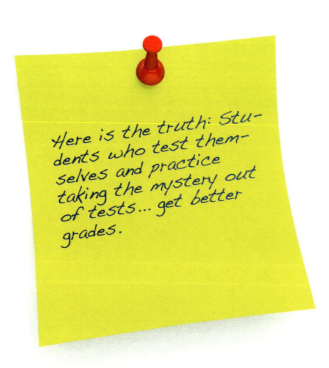

Here is the truth: Students who test themselves and practice taking the mystery out of tests... get better grades.

Step 7: Reflecting

You finally have your new phone and have personalized it with your choice of screensaver, color, theme, wallpaper and ringtones. Now get off the phone for a few minutes, sit back, and reflect on the whole experience.

Maybe every once in awhile you remember what life was like without your new cell phone—or if you use up your minutes (because you bought *that* expensive plan!) you might have to suffer through a few days again without it. No problem. You lived years without one before!

Or, after awhile you might even see a new ad and consider an upgrade. Never hurts to dream! Reflecting is part of the learning experience. Don't skip it.

Reflecting

> Am I satisfied with my cell phone choice?
> What might I have done differently?
> What advice would I give a friend who is preparing to buy a cell phone?

That's exactly how your mind REFLECTS on new learning. It puts you back into the experience of learning something new in __XYZ__ class and encourages you to consider your feelings, insights, and reactions to the learning experience.

True learning is a deeply personal experience, so writing down your thoughts is the best way to reflect on what you went through. That way you become aware of how the learning has changed you. Because it has.

Keeping journal notes about what surprised you and which learning tasks you found especially difficult (and how you dealt with those difficulties) will help you become a more self-directed learner.

By improving your learning behaviors, you are improving yourself. Others will notice the difference—and so will you.

Perhaps the most important question you can ask yourself during the REFLECTING Step is, "Now that I have learned all this, why does it matter?" *Glad you asked!*

Pair/Share

Complete the following: As I reflect upon myself as a learner, I will...

Learning that lasts involves giving yourself a reminder that you have accomplished something challenging.

Reflecting is another way of giving yourself a pat on the back for making "smart" self-taught.

A Defining Moment

Learning in school should be as natural as the processes you used to select your cell phone—or any other item important to you.

You only need to LEARN the StudyWhiz MindFrames and USE them in ways that complement your most natural learning style.

Just as one picture frame can totally change the impact of the picture, MindFrames *on you* might look very different from MindFrames on someone else. It's all good.

Oprah Winfrey tells the story of what she calls a "defining moment." When she was in third grade, her teacher complimented her in front of the entire class about a book report she had written. Then the teacher told other teachers what a good job she had done. In this, Oprah's "defining moment," she learned that if she worked hard and did well, people would remember and value her.

A "defining moment" is a moment that stands out in your life. It's a moment that has made a positive difference. It's a moment that you would have been sorry to miss. Even more, it's a moment that has reshaped the very person you are.

When you turn this page, you will begin a journey that may well change your life. One thing is certain: The decision to become a self-directed learner **will be** a "defining moment" in your life.

Oops, excuse me, my cell phone is beeping. Someone must be texting me! Hey, it's a text message with a picture attached. Here it comes . . .

The *picture* is one of a star, *framed* in gold.

And the message reads:
The star and the gold R U!

It's time to show what you can do!

Create your own icon for each Mindframe and write what that Mindframe means to you.

Use free association. Jot down any ideas that come to you.

Previewing

Naming

Connecting

Recapping

Constructing

Self-Testing

Reflecting

Previewing means...

Naming means...

Connecting means...

Recapping means...

Constructing means...

Self-Testing means...

Reflecting means...

SECTION 2

Previewing

Naming

Connecting

Recapping

Constructing

Self-Testing

Reflecting

MindFrame: Previewing

Big Idea: Previewing Sets the Stage for Self-Directed Learning

IntroView

Advertisers are great at getting you to PREVIEW! Think about your favorite cereal. Now picture the cereal box. Do you recall that some words and objects stand out? They grab your attention by being bigger, bolder, or centered to catch your eye.

Cereal packages also capture your attention by advertising a "FREE" prize inside. Yet the prize's picture on the box is usually much larger and cooler than what you find inside. Cereal eaters just come to expect it.

Just as advertisers use size, color, and layout to entice you and your money, textbook publishers use similar techniques to draw attention to important concepts.

> When your mind sees something new—like a catchy ad or a new chapter—it creates a frame for this "newness" by searching for clues that capture your attention and focus your energy. Experts call this search for clues previewing.

When learning, it helps to preview (scan) for the hardest content, important details, bullet points, vocabulary, charts, etc. Today's colorful textbooks are rich with sidebars, pictures, and organizers. Your mind will store away the information that is more interesting, more important, and more complicated—to you.

By the way, have you ever seen a textbook that says, "Don't worry about this information? It's not important?" I doubt it. Textbook writers present everything as important, because they expect learners to organize the content for themselves.

Previewing also involves making predictions about how to organize new information. Preview and predict: Two partnering words that sound similar. (Say them to yourself a few times.)

To really understand a textbook, learners must know how to read between the lines—using clues like bold print, italics, color changes, graphs, boxes, photos and lists. It's like having a silent conversation with the text that will jump start the learning process. (Are you thinking, "Am I really supposed to talk to my textbook?" Of course. Anyone who really knows how to learn does! Think of what you have been missing.) This "conversation"—your speaking to the book and its speaking to you—is part of the secret to previewing.

Imagine putting together a puzzle without seeing the picture on the box. Unless you can see the picture (call it a map), it will be more difficult to get that puzzle together—unless you are a puzzle genius or have all year.

The same is true of learning. Self-directed learners recognize that creating a personal map (picture) for organizing their learning is essential. There is such a maze of information in nearly every textbook chapter that you need that map to get you through. But it's your map to make, and you can't do it without previewing.

Previewing is the first step in taking control of your learning—and some think it could be the most important.

How Do You Stack Up Right Now as a Self-Directed Learner Who Knows How to Preview?

Previewing: I make a mental map before learning.

1. I use sticky notes to mark important information in my text such as **Bold Words,** pictures, and color changes.

   ☐ **Never**   ☐ **Sometimes**   ☐ **Often**

2. I look for ideas and information that I already know and try to predict what the author is trying to say about the topic.

   ☐ **Never**   ☐ **Sometimes**   ☐ **Often**

3. I make a short list of ideas and information that look especially important, to remind myself to spend time thinking about what they mean

   ☐ **Never**   ☐ **Sometimes**   ☐ **Often**

4. I have an inner conversation with the author about questions before I even begin to learn the material.

   ☐ **Never**   ☐ **Sometimes**   ☐ **Often**

Pair/Share

With a partner, discuss the Learning Survey.

Did You Know?

The Meaning of Color

Imagine a colorless world:

> Traffic signs, billboards, and marquis all in black and white.
>
> Television and computer screens in black and white.
>
> Every sport team in black and white uniforms.
>
> All food products in black and white packaging.

You live in a color-drenched world (unless you are color blind, that is.) Color is used to identify things quickly, make objects stand out, express ourselves, and even keep us safe. In fact, researchers say that the human eye can distinguish over one million colors. (Some say over seven million!)

Colors affect our reactions to the environment. When we see a yellow floor sign, a yellow road sign, or a yellow taped off area, we usually slow down. (Can you think of other ways yellow affects behaviors?)

Colors also affect our moods and emotions. Some colors make us hungry, others soothe. Some might even make you smile. Think about all the colors you see in a fast food place, a doctor's office, even your own bedroom.

Your eyes cannot process every object at one time. That's why authors and illustrators work together to use color as a tool to help students focus, concentrate, and learn. And did you know that color stimulates the brain?

The Meaning of Color Throughout the Ages

Color	Color's Impact on Primitive Man (Luscher, 1948)	Color during the Middle Ages (Edwards, 1999)	Modern-Day Color Influences (Hewlewtt-Packard, 1999)
Dark Blue	quiet, passive	purity, sincerity	tranquility, intuitive, trustworthy, peace, harmony, security
Light Blue	coolness, calm		quiet, coolness, calm, softness, purity, understanding, peace

Green	food	youth, fertility	generosity, nature, envy, fertility, good luck, success, hope
Yellow	hope, activity		enthusiasm, playful, optimism, joy, action, hope, sunshine
Orange	strength	strength, endurance	happy, courage, ambition, fun, balance, organic, warm
Red	excitement, attack	courage, zeal	energy, optimism, passion, dynamic, intense, danger
Pink			friendly, love, compassion, sweetness, faithful, softness
Purple		royalty, high birth	spirituality, royalty, mystery, wisdom, independence, wealth
Gold		honor	illumination, wisdom, wealth
Brown	restful, neutral	common	stability, earthy, reliable, masculine, comfort, simplicity
Grey	free from stimulus, no-man's land		neutral, corporate, practical, cold, hard
White		fate, purity	
Black		grief, penitence	

Visual Impact, Visual Teaching – Timothy Ganwer, 2005

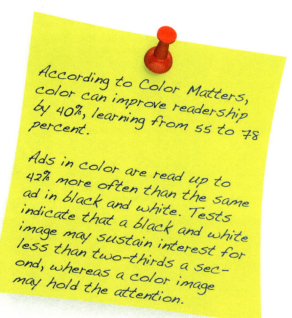

According to Color Matters, color can improve readership by 40%, learning from 55 to 78 percent.

Ads in color are read up to 42% more often than the same ad in black and white. Tests indicate that a black and white image may sustain interest for less than two-thirds a second, whereas a color image may hold the attention.

Practice Makes Permanent

—David Sousa

Previewing Tips

Successful students don't just jump in and start learning. They preview. Just as a movie preview hopes you'll get interested in an upcoming movie, your chapter preview should get you interested in the chapter.

General Tips

- Skim and scan the chapter's layout.
- Notice all the visuals—graphs, charts, pictures, etc.
- Make some predictions about what you will be expected to learn.
- Note what you already know.

Good students make it a habit to preview. In doing so, their brains are geared up for maximum learning with minimal stress.

Features of Informational Text

Here are excellent stopping points in your skimming and scanning "preview":

We are what we repeatedly do. Excellence, then, is not an act, but a habit.

—Aristotle

Table of Contents – "Where is all this information taking me?" If this is the first time you are previewing, don't forget the table of contents! The table of contents allows you to quickly scroll through the topics in the chapters in the order in which they appear, giving you the "big picture" of where the author is taking you. It's like the "main menu" on a DVD.

Print Features
Print features inform you how the author has organized information and guide you in capturing important ideas and details.

Self-directed learners look for and read: titles, headings, subheadings, bold print, italics, repeated words, captions – usually under visual or graphic features, colored print, font size/changes, numbers, bullets, side bars – information in the margins.

Graphic features
Graphic features convey key information in a deeper way than text alone.

Self-directed learners look carefully at: charts, diagrams, graphs, tables, time lines, maps, boxes, lists.

Visual features
You've heard the saying, "a picture is worth a thousand words." Visual features relay information that words alone can't say. Visuals help the reader better understand relationships that exist between size of people, places and things, and living creatures that words and numbers can't do alone.

Self-directed learners look carefully at:
* Pictures/illustrations
* Photographs
* Cartoons
* Drawings
* Paintings
* Sketches

Previewing in Action

Good PREVIEWING, as you now know, gives you a bird's-eye view of what you're going to learn BEFORE you actually start. That doesn't mean you PREVIEW only the first day of school or the opening lesson of any unit. A self-directed learner often PREVIEWS before each class period and always before reading a new section.

Don't be fooled into thinking that words are all you pay attention to during PREVIEWING. In fact, you begin previewing before you even read the first word by being aware of spatial and formatting clues, such as how the author arranged the information on the page. Your eyes are looking for clues in how the text is laid out. When everything is equal, it is harder for the brain to recognize differences.

Our world provides clues based upon differences in the proportion and size of things and how they fit together. Authors do, too.

Most people see these clues without much thought. What makes a self-directed learner special is that he or she takes these clues and does something with them.

> You too can create visual prompts that will let you actually think about your own thinking. The message here is this: You can read *MORE THAN WORDS*.

Give it a try. Whether you are surveying a textbook chapter or taking notes as your teacher talks, read or notice every clue you possibly can. It's a skill you have to practice. Then your mind can use these clues to make sense of things. Plus, it's fun!

Each person PREVIEWS for something different. One self-directed learner will look first for interesting things. Another will focus on what seems important. Still others will search for what looks familiar or puzzling. Together these four clues—interesting, important, familiar, puzzling—provide a framework for preparing to learn.

Previewing is like taking a sightseeing tour of the upcoming chapter. It will give you a hint as to what the author thinks is important, while also providing a sense of how the chapter is organized.

Finally, previewing will help you learn more about yourself as a learner. Remember "Smart is Self-Taught" Knowing how your brain pays attention is a valuable key to expanding your "learning radar screen" to make meaningful learning more likely.

In the exercise below, you will practice picking out the significant clues to learning. You will begin to make what's important part of your thinking process. And, you will have a head start on teaching *yourself* to be smarter. Again, **smart** is self-taught.

Show You Know

Directions: Scan the pages of the text presented here. Let your eyes search the text for important clues that will help you get the "big picture" of what this chapter is about and how it hangs together.

There are no rules for how fast you should scan the pages, nor which pages to investigate. Let your intuition guide you, since it is connected to the smartest part of your brain.

The Middle Ages

The period from about A.D. 500 to about 1400 is known as the Middle Ages. During the early Middle Ages, invasion and war were common. Without Roman armies, people had to find other means of defending themselves.

Feudalism A new kind of government evolved during the Middle Ages. Kings and queens divided their lands among warrior nobles. In return, nobles promised to fight for the ruler when asked. This system of rule by lords who ruled their lands but owed loyalty and military service to a monarch is called feudalism (FYOOD 'l ihz uhm).

At the top of feudal society stood the king and the most powerful lords. Next came the lesser nobles. Most people in feudal society were peasants who farmed the lord's lands and could not leave the land without the lord's permission.

Viewing History

Peasants and Lords

In the Middle Ages, it was the peasants' duty to farm the lord's lands. The lord in his magnificent castle had the duty of protecting the peasants. **Making Predictions** Based on this painting from France in the early 1400s, and the information on the Middle Ages, what problems do you think could arise between peasant and lord?

Daily Life Feudal life revolved around the manor, which included the lord's castle and the lands around it. Manor lands might include several villages.

Each manor was self-sufficient. That is, people made almost everything they needed. Life for peasants was hard. They struggled to produce enough food just to survive.

The most powerful force was the Roman Catholic Church. It ruled more than religious life. The Church owned large amounts of land and was the source of education. The clergy were often the only people who could read and write. Because of their efforts, much of the learning from the ancient world was preserved.

By about A.D. 900, life began to change. Peasants used new methods of farming to produce more food. Warfare declined and trade began to grow. Slowly, people began to look beyond their isolated villages.

The Crusades The pace of change increased between 1100 and 1300 in part because of the Crusades. The Crusades were a series of wars fought by Christians to control the Holy Land. The Holy Land included Jerusalem and the other places where Jesus had lived and taught. Muslims had controlled this region for centuries.

During the Crusades, tens of thousands of Christians journeyed to the Middle East. Fighting between Christians and Muslims continued for almost 200 years. Christians won some victories. But in the end, they failed to win control of the Holy Land.

Growth of Trade The Crusades had important effects on Europe, however. Crusaders traveled beyond their villages

Chapter 2 *Before the First Global Age*

and came into contact with other civilizations. In the Middle East, they tasted new foods, such as rice, oranges, dates, and new spices. They saw beautiful silks and woven rugs.

Europe had traded with the Middle East for many years before the Crusades. However, returning Crusaders demanded more of the Asian foods, spices, silks, and rugs. Italian merchants realized that people would pay high prices for such goods. They outfitted ships and increased trade with the Muslim world.

New Tools for Navigation Trade brought new knowledge. From the Muslim world, Europeans acquired sailing skills and the magnetic compass. Muslims had earlier adopted the magnetic compass from the Chinese. The special needle of the compass always pointed north, which helped ships stay on course.

Another useful instrument was the astrolabe (AS troh layb), which helped sailors determine their latitude while at sea. These new instruments let Europeans sail far out to sea, beyond sight of land. By 1500, Portugal had taken the lead in this new overseas travel.

The Renaissance Expands Horizons

Increased trade and travel made Europeans eager to learn more about the wider world. Scholars looked in monastery libraries for manuscripts of ancient Greek and Roman works. Some traveled to the Muslim world, where many ancient works had been preserved.

As scholars studied ancient learning, they began to make their own discoveries. They produced new books on art, medicine, astronomy, and chemistry. This great burst of learning was called the Renaissance (REHN uh sahns), a French word meaning rebirth. It lasted from the late 1300s until the 1600s.

A new invention, the printing press, helped to spread Renaissance learning. A German printer named Johannes Gutenberg (GOOT uhn berg) is credited with this invention in the 1430s. Before then, books were scarce and costly because each was copied by hand. With the printing press, large numbers of books could be produced quickly and at a low cost. Soon more people began to read, and learning spread more quickly.

The Search for New Trade Routes During the Renaissance, trade brought new prosperity. European rulers began to increase their power. In England and France, kings and queens tried to bring powerful feudal lords under their control. In Spain and Portugal,

Portuguese Routes of Exploration

Key
- - - → Bartholomeu Dias, 1487–1488
——→ Vasco Da Gama, 1497–1499

GEOGRAPHY Skills

New technologies and new skills allowed Portuguese sailors to make historic voyages along the coast of Africa and across the Indian Ocean to India.

1. **Location** On the map locate (a) Portugal, (b) Cape of Good Hope, (c) Indian Ocean.

2. **Movement** Describe the route taken by Da Gama.

3. **Critical Thinking Drawing Inferences** Why do you think the Cape of Good Hope was an important landmark to sailors?

Viewing History

An African View of the Portuguese

The ivory carving above was done by an African artisan in the 1500s.
Drawing Inferences *How do you think Africans perceived the Portuguese?*

Christian monarchs drove out Muslim rulers, who had governed there for centuries.

Rulers in England, France, Spain, and Portugal were eager to increase their wealth. They saw the great profits that could be made through trade. However, Muslim and Italian merchants controlled the trade routes across the Mediterranean Sea. So, Western Europe's leaders began hunting for other routes to Asia.

European rulers also looked to Africa as a source of riches. Tales of Mansa Musa's wealth had created a stir in Europe, but no one knew the source of African gold.

Portuguese Voyages Portugal was an early leader in the search for a new trade route to Asia and for the source of African gold. In the early 1400s, Prince Henry, known as Henry the Navigator, encouraged sea captains to sail south along the coast of West Africa. Realizing that Portugal needed better navigators to accomplish the task, he set up an informal school to teach sailors techniques of navigation and the art of shipbuilding.

Under Henry's guidance, the Portuguese designed a new type of ship, the caravel (KAR uh vehl). With triangular sails and a steering rudder, caravels could be sailed into the wind. Portuguese caravels stopped at many places along the coast of West Africa. They traded cloth, silver, textiles, and grain for gold, ivory, and slaves.

Slowly, Portuguese explorers ventured farther south, hoping to find a sea route around Africa to the rich spice trade of Asia. In 1488, Bartolomeu Dias reached the southern tip of Africa.

Nine years later, in 1497, Vasco da Gama rounded the Cape of Good Hope at the southern tip of Africa. He then sailed up the coast of East Africa and across the Indian Ocean to India. The Portuguese pushed on to the East Indies, the islands of Southeast Asia and the source of valuable spices.

★ ★ ★ Section 4 Assessment ★ ★ ★

Recall
1. **Identify** Explain the significance of (a) Crusades, (b) Renaissance, (c) Johannes Gutenberg, (d) Prince Henry.
2. **Define** (a) salvation, (b) missionary, (c) direct democracy, (d) republic, (e) feudalism, (f) manor, (g) astrolabe.

Comprehension
3. Describe one tradition from Judaism and Christianity that influenced later Europeans.
4. What were three ideas that Europeans learned from ancient Greece and Rome?
5. How did the Crusades help bring changes to Europe?
6. Why did Renaissance rulers in Western Europe want to find new routes to Asia?

Critical Thinking and Writing
7. **Exploring the Main Idea** Review the Main Idea statement at the beginning of this section. Then, identify reasons for the European exploration of North America.
8. **Drawing Conclusions** Write an editorial explaining whether you think the Crusades were a success or a failure.

ACTIVITY

Writing a Diary You are a sailor on Vasco da Gama's voyage of 1497. With a partner, write two different diary entries that express your hopes and fears about the voyage.

Now answer the following questions:

Previewing in Action

Use of Color

Does the textbook use color to draw your attention to specific words or images in the chapter?

Why do you think the author selected these specific words or images to print in a different color? Do you see a pattern in the colors?

Select at least three places in the text where the words or images are in color. Try to explain why these words and images were colored differently.

Words in **Bold**

Did you notice any words in the chapter that were written in **bold**? (**Bold** print is used to attract attention or create a forceful expression.)

List some words that are in **bold** and decide what these words have in common. (Select **bold** words from different sections of the chapter. Pick the ones you think are most important.)

List 5 important **bold** words here:

1. _____
2. _____
3. _____
4. _____
5. _____

If you are with peers, compare your choices. **Smart** means learning from each other.

Your brain secretly knows why these words are written in **bold**. It just isn't telling you.

Smart is what you do. And here it means making your thoughts visible—that is, *real*. The trick to making **smart** self-taught is to pay special attention to **bold** words early in the learning process. When **bold** words pop up, your brain speaks to you and says, "Pay attention here. You probably will need to know this."

Graphs and Pictures

Select one graph or picture and explain why this graph or picture is particularly important to the meaning of this chapter.

I selected the graph or picture on page_____. I think this illustration is designed to help me better understand the information it describes because...

Boxed Summaries and Lists
Select one boxed summary or list and describe what it tells you:

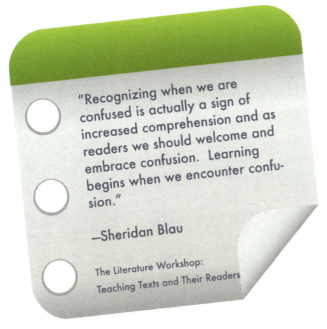

"Recognizing when we are confused is actually a sign of increased comprehension and as readers we should welcome and embrace confusion. Learning begins when we encounter confusion."

—Sheridan Blau

The Literature Workshop: Teaching Texts and Their Readers

Previewing in Action Using Your Own Text

Now use a chapter in a text you are studying and complete the following:

Previewing Practice

Looks Important
G2 of interphase
prophase
metaphase
anaphase
telophase
cytokinesis

Looks Interesting
Spindle formation how daughter cells form Greg or Mendell

Looks Familiar
animal cell
plant cell
chromosomes
nucleus

Looks Difficult
prophase
metaphase
anaphase
telophase

Clues:
Bolded letters
Italics
Repeated words
Headings
Color changes
Opening sentences
Numbers
Illustrations
Graphs
Photos
Boxed summaries
Lists

TOPIC: Mitosis

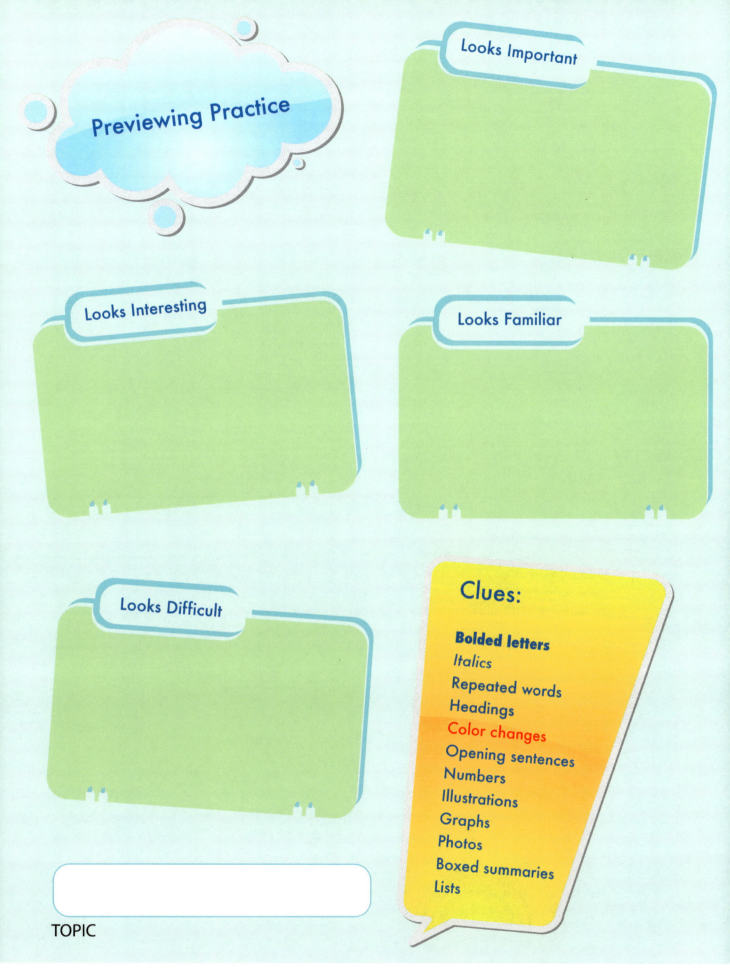

Major Headings

Headings are introductory lines which indicate what the next passage will be about. Count the headings in the chapter and make a list of the ones that you know nothing about or that are the most difficult for you to understand.

> **Noticing what might be difficult to learn (for you) is an essential prerequisite to meaningful learning.**

There are _____ major headings in this chapter.

The three that describe information that I believe will be difficult for me to learn are:

1. _____

2. _____

3. _____

Opening Sentences

Opening sentences, those first sentences after each major heading, give essential clues to the organization and "gist" of the chapter. Read each opening sentence in order for one major section of the chapter and complete the following:

> In this chapter I am going to learn about. . .

You now have a framework for thinking about how the information fits together. You also have a sense of what to expect, and you should even have a sense of what you are going to learn.

Touring through a chapter before you take notes or study the information will tap into your brain's ability to learn quicker and more efficiently.

You are already making **smart self-taught.**

Skimming the Text and Getting the Gist

Don't stop there. You can do even more to prepare yourself for learning from the text. Successful learners take it one step further. Before reading the new material, they skim the text.

First and Last Sentence

Successful learners try to gather information from the first sentence of the page or passage and the last sentence of the passage. The opening sentence often highlights what the passage will be about. The last sentence often provides a reminder of what was most important.

This preview reading activity provides an opportunity for learners to predict the middle of the paragraph in ways that indicate that they are on the right track. This is yet another way to develop a sense of confidence that, as a learner I have what it takes to be successful!

Or, if your prediction was close, perhaps this is a golden opportunity to develop your ability to preview and do better next time. Ask your friends how they predicted the middle of the paragraph. Learn from them. By sharing your thoughts, learners think about their thinking in ways that deepens learning.

First and Last Paragraph

Reading the first and last sentence may not always be enough. Often self-directed learners preview by reading the first and last paragraph of a particularly difficult section of a text to get an even deeper understanding of the content. Like the skimming strategy, the first paragraph usually introduces the big picture or main idea of the text; the last paragraph usually sums it up. Also like the skimming strategy, the prediction is where the learning takes place.

Getting the Gist is a pre-learning strategy that will help you make better sense of what you are reading. First pick a passage of the text you have to read. Now write the first sentence on "Opening Sentence". Next write the last sentence in the box called "Closing Sentence". Do not read the passage yet. In the space in the middle, write your prediction of what the passage is about.

After writing your prediction, read the passage and then check in the circle how did you do. Don't forget to fill in the Topic Box and the Page Number Box for future reference.

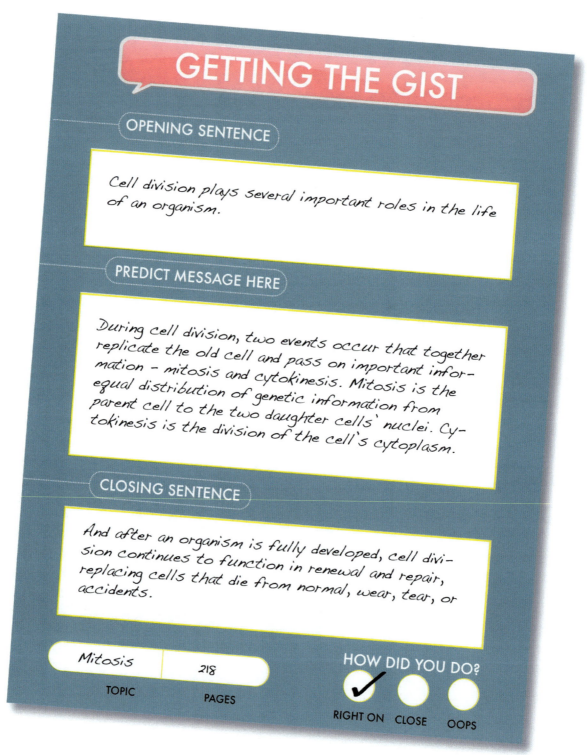

GETTING THE GIST

OPENING SENTENCE

PREDICT MESSAGE HERE

CLOSING SENTENCE

TOPIC | PAGES

HOW DID YOU DO?

RIGHT ON | CLOSE | OOPS

Word Wall

The **Word Wall** is a great way to organize and keep track of the important words you will need to learn. You can use the Word Wall in several ways. One strategy is to go through the chapter and list on the Word Wall words you think will be on your test. Later, when you have learned the word, put a check in the little circle on the top of the word box.

After the test, go back and check the words that actually were on your test. This will help you know if you are improving your ability to second-guess the facts to learn. It's another way that smart is self-taught.

You can also use the Word Wall to find vocabulary words you already know and put them on your Word Wall. This will save time when you study.

Finally, list the words you think will be on your test on the Word Wall.

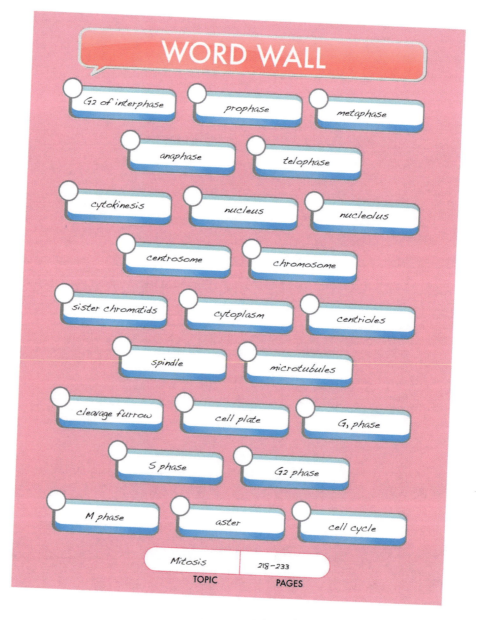

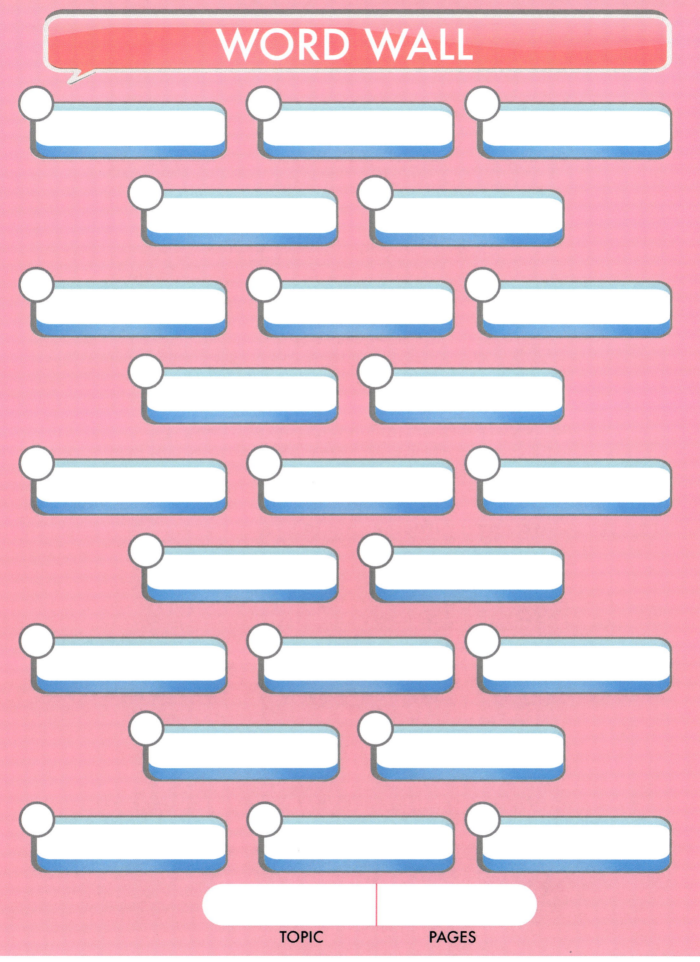

Extending Your Word Wall Words

Have you ever thought of words as tools? You couldn't read, write, think or talk without them! That's why the number of words we own (understand) can impact our ability to think, write, formulate, learn, and communicate ideas.

The Word Wall helps you gather and select important words on the topic and themes you are learning about. But it is important to make those words your "own" so you can use them now and for future learning.

Word Wall Flashcards

Flashcards can help you deal with new or confusing words. Simply writing your Word Wall words on individual note cards allows you to define the word on the back of the card. With the words on individual cards, you can organize and reorganize them into like categories, themes, similarities, sequence of events, hierarchy of importance, etc., as you continue your journey through the MindFrames.

Remember, the brain seeks patterns! The more connections you make, the more likely the words will become your own—which means you know what they mean and can use them yourself.

If You Are Having Trouble, Try This!

There are four degrees or stages of knowing a word:

1. I have never seen or heard the word.
2. I have seen or heard the word, but I do not know what it means.
3. I recognize the word and could use it in limited contexts.
4. I know the word and can use it: multiple meanings, multiple uses, contexts, word forms.

Still having problems previewing or deciding where to look for clues? If so, ask yourself the following:

— Do I know why I need to learn this information?

If you are not motivated to learn, previewing may not be given the attention and energy it deserves. If this is the case, make sure you know "why" you are being asked to learn this information. Sometimes it's a skill or concept you find boring but need to understand first before applying it to something more enjoyable later.

— Am I asking questions before and during the preview?

Sometimes learners jump right in, forgetting to ask themselves what they already know about the topic. Once this is answered, it is time to start asking "smart" questions about the text itself. Do I see words I know? How do the pictures add to what I already know about this topic? What do the colors on this chart represent? What text features do I see that guide me to where I should pay more attention?

—Am I connecting the information and clues to what I already know about the topic?

When you read to learn, you are actually re-writing the text as you read it. We all bring different background experiences and knowledge to the text. We mesh our background knowledge and experiences with the author's words to create, or write, meaning. Make sure you are allowing thinking time to make these connections.

Lessons Learned

In this chapter on Previewing you learned that when your mind approaches something new, it frames this "newness" by searching for clues that it can use to focus attention and direct energy. When previewing a text, self-directed learners scan what they are trying to learn and notice ways that some things are marked as important and others as less important.

You also learned that Previewing helps you make predictions about the content of the text and plan how the text needs to be studied. Students who preview decide what to read first, where they may need to slow down and concentrate more deeply, and where the most important information or details may be located.

In Your Own Words

Complete the following sentence: Previewing will help me become a more self-directed learner because…

To preview what I am going to learn, I will:

1.

2.

3.

4.

Coming Next

Naming

Self-directed learners pay special attention to how things are different. For example, the sun and the moon are important to life on earth yet they are different in many ways. That's why they don't have the same names. Once something important is seen as different from another thing, it gets a name. We use names to frame the way we describe important people, ideas and things and to learn more about how they fit into our world.

Previewing and **Naming** make taking in and learning new information easier.

MindFrame 2 is all about Naming. Before you study this chapter, be sure to PREVIEW it.

> In what ways is it like PREVIEWING?
> How is it different?
> In your skimming, what do you see that might be new?
> Do you see any content that you've had before?
> What interests you right from the start?

Okay, now get set for more tips that could change your success in school . . . now and forever!

MindFrame: Naming

Big Idea: Learning Involves Paying Special Attention to Differences

IntroView

Naming is how we categorize things so that we can think about them.

Over 200 years ago Noah Webster published the first dictionary: *A Compendious Dictionary of the English Language*—with a mere 37,000 entries. Each entry was a name and definition of something considered important. Today's dictionary contains over 301,100 entries. Next year it will have more!

So, how *does* a word become part of the language?

Each year, the Merriam-Webster, Oxford English, and other dictionaries have to decide which new words should be named and defined. To do this, editors spend hours reading and marking a wide variety of published materials that include books, newspapers, magazines, and electronic publications. They look for words that regularly appear either in print, on TV, over the Internet or merely have simply been around long enough to attain the status of common usage. If a word shows up often enough, the editors consider adding it to their dictionary.

Look at this list of interesting words. (Are you surprised at how long some of them have been around?) Check the ones you've heard before:

- [ ] **ginormous** (adj) 1948: gigantic + enormous, extremely large

- [ ] **mouse potato** (n) 1993: slang: a person who spends a great deal of time using a computer

- [ ] **ringtone** (n) 1983: the sound made by a cell phone to signal an incoming call

- [ ] **spyware** (n) 1994: software that is installed in a computer without the user's knowledge and transmits information about the user's computer activities over the Internet

- [ ] **biodiesel** (n) 1986: a fuel that is similar to diesel fuel and is derived from usually vegetable sources (e.g. soybean oil)

- [ ] **soul patch** (n) 1991: a small growth of beard under a man's lower lip

- [ ] **supersize** (v) 1994: to increase considerably the size, amount, or extent of

- [ ] **labelmate** (n) 1981: a singer or musician who records for the same company as another

- [ ] **wave pool** (n) 1977: a large swimming pool equipped with a machine for making waves

- [ ] **drama queen** (n) 1979: a person given to often excessively emotional performances or reactions

- [ ] **unibrow** (n) 1988: a single continuous brow resulting from the growing together of eyebrows

- [ ] **qigong** (n) 1974: an ancient Chinese healing art involving meditation, controlled breathing, and movement exercises

- [ ] **big-box store** (n) 1990: of, relating to, or being a large chain store having a boxlike structure

- [ ] **aquascape** (n) 1954: 1. a scenic view of a body of water 2. an area having a natural or constructed aquatic feature (as a pond or fountain)

- [ ] **coqui** (n) 1903: a small chiefly nocturnal aboreal frog native to Puerto Rico that has a high-pitched call and has been introduced into Hawaii and southern Florida

- [ ] **sandwich generation** (n) 1987: a generation of people who are caring for their aging parents while supporting their own children

- [ ] **bling-bling also bling** (n) 1999: flashing jewelry worn esp. as an indication of wealth; broadly: expensive and ostentatious possessions

- [ ] **bodyboard** (n) 1982: a short surfboard on which the rider lies prone

- [ ] **degenderize** (vt) 1987: to eliminate any reference to a specific gender in (as a word, text, or act)

- [ ] **dreamscape** (n) 1948: a dreamlike, usually surrealistic scene; also: a painting of a dreamscape

- [ ] **empty suit** (n) 1950: an ineffectual executive

- [ ] **google** (v) 2001: to use the Google search engine to obtain information about (as a person) on the World Wide Web

- [ ] **text messaging** (n) 1982: the sending of short text messages electronically esp. from one cell phone to another

Thinking Practice

Write a creative paragraph in the box using as many words from this list as you can:

Long, long ago, far, far away, there lived a drama queen...

How Do You Stack Up Right Now as a Self-Directed Learner Who Knows How to Name?

NAMING: I make what is important, important.

1. I use my dictionary or search the internet to learn more about words I don't know.

☐ Never ☐ Sometimes ☐ Often

2. I use a special note-taking method that makes it easier to take notes in class.

☐ Never ☐ Sometimes ☐ Often

3. I write class notes in my own words and use different symbols to highlight what I am learning.

☐ Never ☐ Sometimes ☐ Often

4. I go back after class and revise my notes, add questions, and use a highlighter to make my notes come alive.

☐ Never ☐ Sometimes ☐ Often

Did You Know?

Think about words like **soulpatch**, **supersize**, and **drama queen**. These labels show their differences from other things. Once something is seen as different, a new **name** is needed.

Your brain retrieves information from your memory by using a name. In other words, anytime you search your memory for information you need a name to find this information.

> **Pair/Share**
>
> Discuss with a partner preferred Naming learning strategies.

During a test, your performance will be only as good as the names you know and the differences you learned. Self-generated material is easier to recall, especially when you have written the study notes yourself. After all, you took the time to write it all down.

Experts call this process of taking information from different sources and putting it in your own words *re-coding.* Students call it taking notes!

Depending on where you are—in your bedroom studying, at the mall, at a sporting

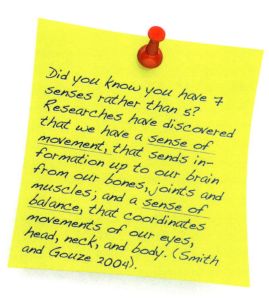

Did you know you have 7 senses rather than 5? Researches have discovered that we have a sense of movement, that sends information up to our brain from our bones, joints and muscles; and a sense of balance, that coordinates movements of our eyes, head, neck, and body. (Smith and Gouze 2004).

event—at any given moment your brain receives between 50 to 2,000 sensory messages. (Sensory messages are anything that hit the eyes, nose, ears, mouth, and skin—in other words, your senses!)

Stop and think about the sensory inputs you are receiving at this very moment.

What can you see?

Hear?

Can you taste or smell anything?

Are you cold? Hot? Comfortable?

If you think about it, the amount of sensory input your brain must sort through in order to focus on the task at hand is amazing!

When your brain tries to make sense of input, it goes through three main steps:

> 1. **Receptive** step = Taking in sensory information from the environment
> 2. **Processing** step = Organizing and storing information for memory
> 3. **Expressive** step = Sending a message to your muscles, causing you to act

In school, these steps are the natural cycle of note taking, also called **naming**:

First, you receive information from reading, a lecture, a demonstration, a video, etc. That's **RECEPTIVE**.

Then, you recode and blend the information with what you already know. That's **PROCESSING**.

Finally, you act on the new information or learning by summarizing, filling in the missing parts, and translating it for storage as **semantic memory.** (*Semantic memory* includes facts, figures, labels, names of things, and events–things that show up on multiple choice questions. And that's **EXPRESSIVE**.

> You don't know anything clearly unless you can state it in writing.
>
> —Sihayakawa, Language in Thought and Action

Carefully read the quote in the box by Sihayakawa. Do you agree with this? Explain.

Remember that when you're reading an opinion in a textbook, you don't *always* have to agree. That's called *thinking for yourself*.

Textbooks will become much more interesting if you think while you're reading—and sometimes question ideas, opinions, and even facts.

So, again: Is there anything you might "know" that you cannot express in writing? Discuss this. Your ideas are important!

Seeing Naming in Action: Taking Notes from Text

Leaving Tracks

No one can remember everything he or she reads. But, self-directed learners use tools to keep track of their thinking. You will use these same tools over and over—in nearly every subject.

The most common ones are sticky notes, writing in the textbook (if you own it), using a highlighter, taking notes on paper, and making note cards. (Can you think of others?)

These track your thinking. And they come in *really* handy when you're studying for a test!

They will help . . .

- as you sift through information for the most important details

- by reminding you of where you had questions, where you made connections, or where you were confused, and

- later, if you need to add notes or get help from a teacher or peer.

As you work your way through the text, use symbols or codes as short cuts to focus your thinking along the way. Such symbols or codes are commonly called **logo graphics.**

As with notes, your best **logo graphics** will be those you make up yourself. They are like sign posts making your thinking visible—a goal of self-directed learning.

Actually, you use logo graphics all the time. Think about the emoticons you use in text messages and e-mails. Here are a few examples of logo graphics that might be useful as "thought trackers" in your textbook:

 for I got it

 for stop and think

 for I'm confused

Thinking Practice

Now it's your turn to design your own logo graphics. If you're working with a group, don't show yours until the end. It will be fun to compare. (Your group might even want to put some on the board and see if others can guess what the logos represent!)

Okay, create logo graphics for the following:

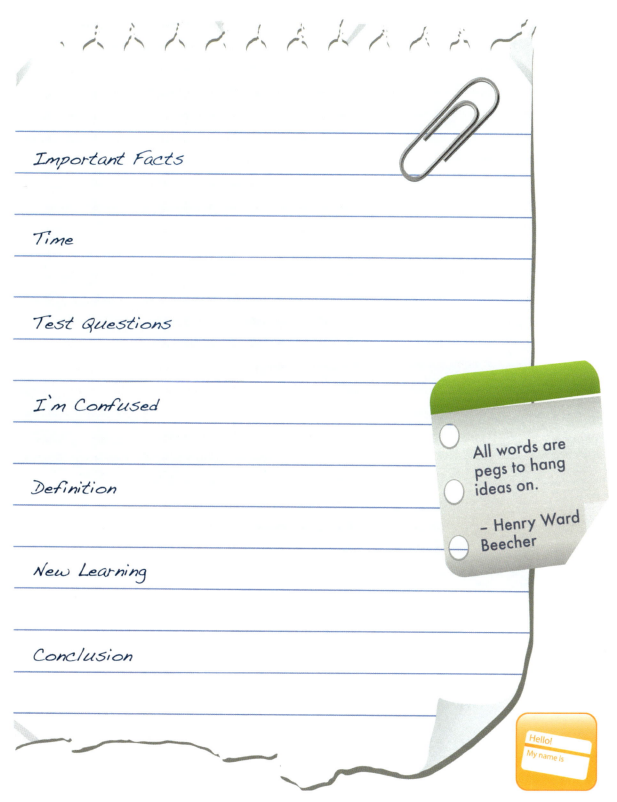

Important Facts

Time

Test Questions

I'm Confused

Definition

New Learning

Conclusion

> All words are pegs to hang ideas on.
>
> – Henry Ward Beecher

Looking For Signal Words

If you're hiking on a wilderness trail and come upon to a rushing river, it's a relief to see a bridge!

Signal words are like bridges, connecting sentences, paragraphs, and ideas to one another. They "signal" that a new or important idea is coming up.

For example, "first" is a signal word because you can expect "second" to follow. Another signal word is "because." When you see that, you have a sense that a reason is coming. As in, *I like reading, because I learn so much.*

Writers use signal words to direct the reader. You will want to become familiar with signal words—clues that help take the mystery out of reading. Self-directed learners are "clue experts."

Study the chart below. The ways writing is often organized are listed in the left column. Descriptions of these techniques are in the middle. And the signal words most commonly used for each writing style are on the right.

(By the way, all through high school and college you will be doing this type of writing—called **expository** writing. So this StudyWhiz section will get you two laps ahead of everyone else. Take some time with the chart—focusing on the signal words.)

It wouldn't be safe on the road without traffic signals!

And, trust me, studying a chapter without **signal words** would make the reading very difficult. Furthermore, be sure to use signal words in your own writing. *(What signal word did I just use? Find a signal word from the chart below and use it to add one more sentence to this paragraph.)*

You are not expected to memorize these signal words, but you'll probably pick up on similarities among them. (I've actually heard of students who photo-copied this list and taped it inside their notebooks. One teacher even taped it to her desk!)

Relationship	Things to keep in mind:	Signal words:	
Time Order and Sequence	Authors use words to help the reader keep track of the order of events. They also use words to help place the reader in a time of the past or the future.	after afterward at first at the present at the same time before earlier eventually formerly finally following immediately in the beginning/end	in the meantime initially last later meanwhile next ... then now presently previously soon subsequently thereafter ultimately
Order of Importance	It's often hard to find the most important ideas in a text. Authors often use signal words to help you focus on the most important ideas.	above all best of all more important most important of greatest importance	of greater importance of greater concern of major concern to begin with worst of all
Conclusion	As a review of what are the major points in a section, the author often paraphrases the section to help the readers pull their thoughts together.	as already stated finally in any case in any event in brief in conclusion to sum up in summary	in short in the end on the whole therefore thus to reiterate in other words
Comparisons	When you compare, you look for similarities ... how things are alike or similar. When authors introduce something new, they often compare it to something else to better help the reader understand.	all as another as well as at the same time besides both by the same token for instance	furthermore in a like manner in the same way just as like likewise same as similarly

Contrast	When you contrast, you look for differences between things or concepts. The author often highlights differences between two or more things after comparisons are used.	although as opposed to but conversely despite difference even though/if however in/by contrast in spite of instead less/more than	nevertheless nonetheless notwithstanding neither … nor on the contrary on the other hand rather regardless though unlike whereas yet
Cause and Effect	To find the **effect**, ask yourself: **"What happened?"** To find the **cause**, ask yourself: **"Why did it happen?"** Even though the cause always happens before the effect, the cause and effect are not always presented in order in the text. The effect may be presented first, even though the cause occurred earlier.	accordingly as as a result because consequently due to for this reason hence if … then	in effect leads to resulting since so therefore thereby thus

Show You Know: Signal Words and Word Roots

Part 1

Refer to the signal words chart. Now, using your own textbook, find six words in a chapter that signal: (Try two for each bullet point below.)

◆ time, order, and sequence

◆ cause and effect

◆ conclusion

Do you notice any patterns here? If so, explain.

Part 2

Using a dictionary, find at least three words that contain the following Greek and Latin roots. List these words in the space provided.

Common Greek and Latin Roots

ROOT	ORIGIN	MEANING	EXAMPLES
aud	Latin	hear	
astro	Greek	star	
bio	Greek	life	
cept	Latin	take	
dict	Latin	speak or tell	
duct	Latin	lead	
geo	Greek	earth	
graph	Greek	write	
ject	Latin	throw	
meter	Greek	measure	
min	Latin	little or small	
mit or mis	Latin	send	
ped	Latin	foot	

phon	Greek	sound	_____
port	Latin	carry	_____
rupt	Latin	break	_____
scrib or script	Latin	write	_____
spect	Latin	see	_____
struct	Latin	build or form	_____
tele	Greek	from afar	_____
tract	Latin	pull	_____
vers	Latin	turn	_____

Diamond, L., & Gutlohn, L. (2006). Vocabulary handbook. Berkeley, CA: Consortium on Reading Excellence; Ebbers, S. (2005). Language links to Latin, Greek, and Anglo-Saxon: Increasing spelling, word recognition, fluency, vocabulary, and comprehension through roots and affixes. Presented at The University of Texas, Austin, TX; and Stahl, S., & Kapinus, B. (2001). Word power: What every educator needs to know about teaching vocabulary. Washington, DC: National Education Association.

Time's up. Count your words. (Did you win?) Now see if you can define the words, using the chart above. And now you may *take your time*.

Common Prefixes

PREFIX	MEANING	EXAMPLES
un-	not, opposite of	unaware, unbelievable, unsure
re-	again	redo, replay
im-, in-, il-, ir-	not	impossible, incapable, illogical, irregular
dis-	not, opposite of	dishonest, disgraceful, discover
en-, em-	cause to	enable, emblaze
non-	not	nonstick, nonfiction, nonexistent
in-, im-	in, into	inject
over-	too much	overtime, overeat
mis-	wrongly	misunderstand, misuse
sub-	under	subsurface, subway

pre-	before	prepay, preschool
inter-	between	international, interact
fore-	before	forethought
de-	opposite of	decaffeinated, dehydrate
trans-	across	transatlantic
super-	above	superhero, supermodel
semi-	half	semiannual, semicolon
anti-	against	antiwar, antisocial
mid-	middle	midyear, midnight
under-	too little	underweight, underpaid

Top 20 prefixes from Carroll, J. B., Davies, P., & Richman, B. (1971). *The American heritage world frequency book.* Boston: Houghten Mifflin; as cited in White, Sowell, & Yanagihara, 1989.

Practice

The race is on! Grab some scratch paper and a pencil. Look in your textbook to find as many words containing the above prefixes as you can. You may use one prefix only five times. Good luck! YOU HAVE 10 MINUTES.

Naming In Action: Taking Class Notes From Lectures

SmartNotes

NAMING transforms what you are learning from your teacher and your textbook into your own words. For your **NAMING practice**, StudyWhiz uses an adaptation of Cornell Notes, a brilliant invention of Dr. Walter Pauk, to help you make learning interactive. This design is called **SmartNotes**—and you'll probably agree they are the smartest notes you've ever seen! (If you take notes like this, you'll be smartest too!)

Study these two pages of **SmartNotes** on mitosis. How do these notes differ from the notes you usually take?

MindFrames in Action

Try taking SmartNotes from your next class lecture. Remember, your SmartNotes must be written in your own words.

Learning to paraphrase is an important element of self-directed learning. Don't forget to leave a space for later editing or adding. Adding color to your symbols also makes your SmartNotes come alive.

Your notes are exactly that—**YOUR** notes! They are a tool for recording your thinking and learning. Just like designing your own website or social networking site, make them your own! Personalize and organize each section in ways that make the most sense to you!

Like this self-directed learner, you start by completing the **Topic Section**. Your topic should be the most important word or words from the section of the book, lecture, overhead or PowerPoint used to get your notes in the first place.

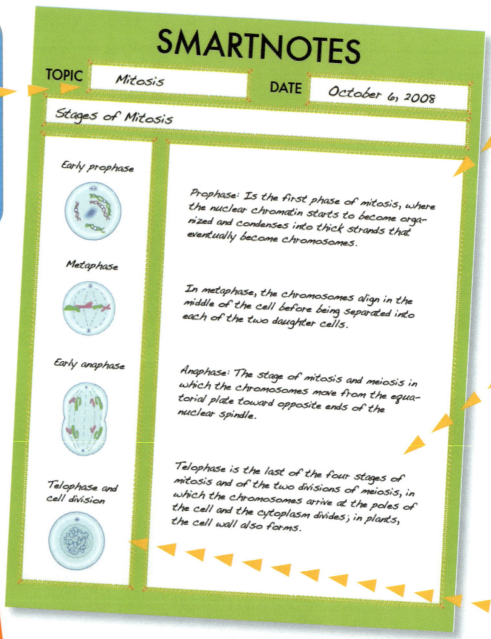

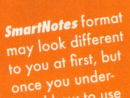

SmartNotes format may look different to you at first, but once you understand how to use it and practice it several times, you will see its value.

Notes Column probably looks most familiar. It's quite a bit like the notes many students take. (Are your notes this neat? Tell the truth now!)

The Notes Column is usually filled in first, especially if you are taking class notes. It provides a space to jot down important events, ideas, people, definitions, formulas, etc.

In this section you should always translate words from your teacher or from printed material into your own words, symbols, and abbreviations. Also page numbers where you got the information and test questions that your teacher mentions. (When he or she says, "You need to know this!" that's the place for a symbol—like a star!)

Hint: Using bullets to organize your information works well here. Bullets are like this:

- (Point one)
- (Point two), etc.

As you are taking notes, make sure to leave some "breathing" room—extra space between main ideas so you can come back later to add more information or a question, if need be.

Spaced out notes are also easier to study. Look up at the SmartNotes again. See how clear they are to read? *(How many times have you taken notes that you couldn't read later? Hmmm? I thought so!)*

Cue Words Column. Here you will place the three or more most important words or phrases relating to your topic—the words that will help you remember what you wrote in your SmartNotes.

Often these words come directly from the book or from your teacher. In the Notes Column you explain these terms in your own words. On both sides, include illustrations, signs, symbols, or anything that will help you remember what you need to know. Doodles even work! (Look at some of the examples above.)

Place your Cue Words directly across from what you have written in the Notes Column. In that way, the Cue Words column provides you with notes of your notes. That's really important when test time rolls along. It's much faster to review with a few key words than to have to reread all your notes over and over.

If you've selected great Cue Words, you can often tell the whole story of what you learned just by looking at those words and your visuals. Cue Words plug directly into your memory and act like magnets to attach other information to them.

Someone else might not understand your notes and pictures, but who cares? As long as *you* do. (Draw a smiley face here if you understand that!)

Set your Purpose and Plan for Note Taking

Think about what you already know about the topic.

If using a textbook, preview the text.

Then determine **why** you are taking these notes.

Think of focus questions to guide your reading, like:

- What do I want (expect) to learn?
- What do I need to understand?
- What do I need to look for?
- What should I be listening for?

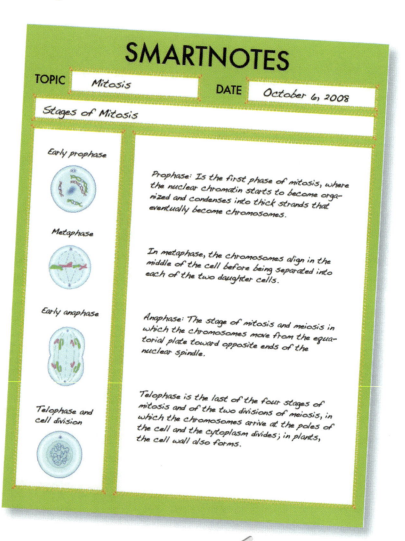

> Obviously you may need several pages to complete all the notes from one lecture or assignment.

SMARTNOTES

TOPIC DATE

Note Layouts

As you saw, the Notes are divided into separate sections.

- Topic – Holds the most important word or words describing the chapter, book, or lecture.

- Notes – Consists of the most important information, ideas, events, people, definitions, and formulas translated into your own words, symbols, abbreviations, and connections.

- Cue Words – Highlights three or more most important words or phrases relating to the topic to help you remember what your SmartNotes are about. They include illustrations, doodles, signs, symbols and other visuals to deepen and cement your understanding. As the saying goes, "A picture paints a thousand words!"

Organize Your Thoughts

Your notes need to **make sense** to you! That's why YOU determine the pattern, what is most important, and how to emphasize aspects of your notes in each section.

Make Them Useful!

You may want to:

- Use information recorded on sticky notes or bookmarks you left in the margins of the text.

- Use bullets, numbers, dashes and symbols

- Identify and organize information into categories (groups, chunks) aligned with headings, subheadings, themes, or order of events.

- Highlight, underline, or circle words or phrases that should stand out.

- Use arrows or connecting lines to show connections or relationships that you have found.

Personalize: Make Them Yours!

Abbreviate! Condense! Your notes are for you to **use.**

Do you shorten words when texting or instant messaging or e-mailing friends? Do the same in your school notes! Condense your notes in ways to help you get more information down in as useful a format as possible.

Here are some ways to do just that:

- **Shorten repetitive or common words:** *info* for information; *thru* for through; *prob* for problem.
- **Use symbols to represent words/ideas:** *w/o* for without, *&* for and; *b/c* for because, *+* for positive or pro, *–* for negative or con; *$* for money.
- **Use acronyms for familiar terms:** *P* for predict; *RMO* for reminds me of; *FMI* for more information.
- **Abbreviate names of people, characters, places, terms:** *GW* for George Washington; *US* for United States; *RW* for Revolutionary War.
- **Cutout unnecessary words.** Use phrases you understand and that make the point.

Learn More? Add More!

Leave space between ideas to add more information later.

If You Are Having Trouble, Try This!

Turn Headings or Titles into Questions during Note Taking

One way to set a purpose for learning is to create questions based on the chapter title, headings, and even subheadings. This helps you learn with *purpose*—to find answers to your questions. For exemple if you were learning about presidential elections in America you might ask "Why are presidents selected by an Electoral college?"

Strategies for Learning New Words

All learners experience confusion at times. Sometimes it's with a word they do not understand. Other times it's a phrase, a longer passage, or a teacher's explanation.

Self-directed learners constantly ask themselves, "Do I understand what I am learning?" They notice *when* and *where* their understanding breaks down, and they use a wide-range of "fix-up strategies" to help them make sense of the confusion.

Here are some fix-up strategies you can use to get unstuck and back on track when the text becomes confusing:

The important thing is not to stop questioning.

– Albert Einstein

Strategies for a Confusing Word

 Think about the text so far and predict what word might make sense or what the word means.

- Read beyond the word and see if the surrounding words or sentences clarify the meaning of the word.
- Look at the word carefully for clues:
  - Is there a part of the word that reminds you of another word that may help with this word's meaning?
  - Is there a prefix, suffix, or root to help you make sense of the word?
- Check the Glossary to see if the word is defined there. If not, look up the word in the dictionary or online.

If you are still confused:

- Ask your teacher, an adult, or a peer for help.
- If no one is around to help, code the location with a sticky note to clarify confusion later.

Strategies for a Confusing Sentence, Passage, or Concept

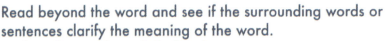

- Go back and reread difficult parts.
- Adjust your reading rate. You may need to slow down.
- Read ahead to clarify meaning.
- Look at visuals and graphics for clues.
- Try to get a mental image.
- Stop and ask yourself what you have already read and how the confusing part may connect.
- Connect what you're reading to your life, other texts you've seen or read, or your knowledge of the world.
- Use text supports such as the Glossary and the Index.

If you're still confused:

- Ask your teacher, an adult, or a peer for help.
- If no one is around to help, code the location with a sticky note to clarify confusion later.
- Look up the concept online, in an encyclopedia, or in another reference book.
- Reread your notes (at least from the previous day and any homework) to set the stage for new connections you can make.

During Class

- Continue to develop new pages of SmartNotes
- Listen for important ideas
- Jot down phrases and key words as possible Cue Words
- Underline, circle, and use your coding symbols
- Use abbreviations
- Translate. Do NOT write down every word you hear
- Record and highlight any suggested test questions
- Put down page numbers from your text where more info can be found

After Class

- Make sure you have filled in the topic and date
- Complete the Cue Words Column
- Add any new material from reading or class discussion to Notes Column
- Use SmartNotes to make Graphic Connectors when appropriate

Where To Find Support in Your Text

Glossary – "I'm stuck! What does that word mean?" If it's important to the topic, you will probably find the word in the glossary at the back of the book. It defines important words on the topics you are reading about. Often, the bold words or words in italics will be defined here.

Index – "Where can I find information on …?" The Index helps you answer just that! It provides a quick way to find information on specific pages in the text. It is almost always in the back of the book.

Lessons Learned

In this chapter on **NAMING** you learned that paying attention to important differences is a key to learning success.

You also learned that humans use names to convey that one idea or thing is different from another and that these names help you organize your thoughts and make sense of your world. These names are what you use to describe and understand things in relation to other things. They are what you use to put the world in order.

Finally, and perhaps most important, names are what you use to retrieve information about the world you have stored in your brain.

One thing you *do not* have to do is teach your brain to think. The human brain is an incredible thinking organ. You can, however, organize the way content is processed to improve learning. In any case, you know that information rarely gets stored if it does not make sense and have meaning to you, the learner.

This is why the SmartNotes system guides learners to paraphrase their notes to meaning and connect them to important cue words (names).

In Your Own Words

Naming strategies can help me become a more self-directed learner because...

To name what I am learning, I will

1.

2.

3.

4.

Coming Next

Connecting

Learning also involves noticing how ideas fit together.

If **NAMING** focuses on differences, **CONNECTING** is all about similarities.

Understanding the similarities and differences among ideas is critical to becoming a more self-directed learner. What this means is that information stored in the brain is locked away in a file that has a name—without the name, no information. The brain retrieves information by differences.

Self-directed learners know the importance of this fact and they use it to their advantage.

The first phase of the natural learning cycle goes like this:

- First, connect to prior knowledge (preview).
- Second, specify how new ideas are different and unique (naming).
- Third, store these names in memory by placing them in similar or related groups (connecting).

MindFrame 3 is all about Connecting. I'm sure you can't wait to PREVIEW this chapter before diving in.

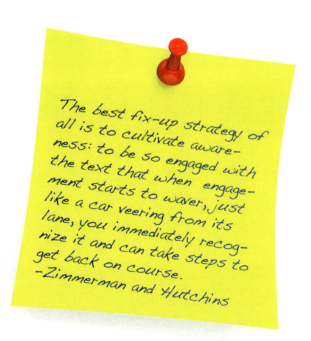

The best fix-up strategy of all is to cultivate awareness: to be so engaged with the text that when engagement starts to waver, just like a car veering from its lane, you immediately recognize it and can take steps to get back on course.
—Zimmerman and Hutchins

MindFrame: Connecting

Big Idea: Learning Also Involves Looking for How Things Fit Together

IntroView

The human brain is a pattern seeker. That's why there are categories everywhere you look. Restaurants, for example: Italian, Mexican, Chinese, all-American steakhouse. Fast food places: burgers, tacos, chicken. Can you add to these lists?

Think about the last time you downloaded your favorite songs from the Internet or walked into a music store to find your favorite artist or group. If you had one CD in mind but would have to read through each available title, that would be hundreds—if not thousands.

However, CD's are grouped in categories by genre (or category) of music, so you can quickly find what you wanted. What are the various music categories that you've seen in stores?

It is the same with buying a book. The shelves are all labeled for your shopping convenience. You can go right where your book fits into (fiction, hobbies, biographies, art, children's books, etc.) and find it quickly.

If you need new athletic shoes, you look for your favorite brand (Nike, Reebok, etc.) or the right sports section (basketball, football, tennis, etc.). Thank goodness for categories and labels!

Learning works much the same way. Your brain stores information in categories, by placing things that are similar together. Then you can "go" right to a specific grouping to find what you want.

> The human brain—like music and books and shoes—categorizes by similarity. Looking for similarities in the information you are learning and chunking that information into categories improves your memory capacity. Basically, the brain's categories help you retrieve information more easily when you need it.

In school, putting related ideas into categories will also help get them into your long-term memory. Long-term memory is background knowledge that you can connect with new knowledge.

Students who look for the connections between ideas and information are learning another important step to becoming a self-directed learner. **Connections** lead to greater levels of understanding. And understanding is the "glue" of the learning process.

Remember: **Smart is self-taught.** This chapter will teach you how to look for connections in your experiences. Connections can come from books, TV, You Tube, people, blogs, or other situations you may encounter. Seeing a connection usually means two things:

1. Your connection probably came from previous knowledge that was meaningful.

2. When CONNECTING, you will begin to see possibilities that reach into many other areas of your life.

Do you think there is a difference between *memorization* and *comprehension*?

Have you ever memorized something in school with no understanding of what it meant? If so, I'm sure that was frustrating.

Memorization involves one specific instance and is often temporary. **Comprehension**, on the other hand, involves making connections that can be used in multiple situations.

That's why when you take a test and the question is in a different form than what you studied, memorization doesn't work so well. Each of the seven MindFrames in StudyWhiz is a comprehension strategy to expand and deepen your understanding.

How Do You Stack Up Right Now As A Self-directed Learner Who Knows How To Connect?

Connecting: I create thinking maps that help me see and talk about what I am learning.

1. I use visual organizers (pictures) to illustrate how important ideas fit together.
   ☐ Never   ☐ Sometimes   ☐ Often

2. I group ideas into categories that help me express my understanding of important ideas.
   ☐ Never   ☐ Sometimes   ☐ Often

3. I create timelines and flow charts that help me remember procedures, dates, and events.
   ☐ Never   ☐ Sometimes   ☐ Often

4. I outline what I am learning in ways that make sense to me.
   ☐ Never   ☐ Sometimes   ☐ Often

Pair/Share

Discuss with a partner preferred Connecting learning strategies.

Did You Know?

You have two main types of long-term memory:

(1) Procedural ("how") memory

(2) Declarative ("what") memory

Procedural memory consists of skills you have learned—such as walking, riding a bike, shooting a basketball. They are skills that you have practiced, so they are now automatic. Now you don't have to consciously think how to keep your balance or move your feet, like when first learning how to walk or ride a bike. These skills are tucked away in your procedural memory.

Your **declarative memory** contains facts, figures, words and events from your past. Remember your first day of middle school? Your last vacation? Your first co-ed (or boy-girl) dance—and the nervous excitement you felt? Many of these declarative memories are personal.

Can you recall the names of the seven continents? The difference between a mammal and a reptile? The number of quarters in a dollar?

These declarative memories are of facts, not necessarily personal. They have been stored away, ready to be retrieved when you need them. Your brain sorts facts, figures, and words into groups, or categories. That's why you probably remembered more words in the activity above once you saw how the words fit into specific categories. You CONNECTED the words. You saw how they fit together!

You also have **working memory**, which is temporary, or not long-term. This place has limited space where you can build, take apart, or rework ideas entering your brain for possible long-term storage. But your working memory can only handle a few items at once. It has what is called a functional limit.

If you "chunk" the information into categories, however, you can increase the number of items your brain can hold in working memory. Then they have a better chance of being stored in long-term memory—just like you want!

Chunking will improve your memory power.

Show You Know: Chunking

Let's give chunking a try. Read the list of words through once quickly, then cover them up.

Now record all the words you remember. How did you do?

Words I remember

_____ _____

_____ _____

_____ _____

_____ _____

_____ _____

_____ _____

_____ _____

_____ _____

Seven is the maximum number of items that researchers say adolescents and adults can usually store in their working memory. Because the words were random, you treated each word as a single item, and your working memory just ran out of functional capability. The good news is that you can increase the number of items within the functional capacity of working memory by using a process called "chunking."

Try the words again, this time chunked into categories!

Words I remember

_____   _____
_____   _____
_____   _____
_____   _____
_____   _____
_____   _____
_____   _____

○ Flowers   Transportation
   rose   airplane
   daffodil   truck
○ iris   car
   tulip   train

○ Light   Writing   Furniture
   light bulb   pen   bed
   firefly   chalk   chair
   star   crayon   table
   matches   pencil   desk

How did you do this time? Was it easier to recall more of the words?

For most students, chunking improves recall.

Three Types of Connections Self-directed Learners Make to Deepen Understanding:

1. **Text to Self:** Connections between the text and the reader's experiences and memories.
2. **Text to Text:** Connections the reader makes between two or more types of texts. The text may be other books, movies, TV shows, familiar stories, etc.
3. **Text to World:** Connections between the text and what the reader knows about the world (facts, problems, information).

MindFrames in Action: Graphic Organizers

Now you're ready to start working on some **Graphic Connectors** to organize your learning in visual ways.

A **Mind Map** creates pictures of what you know using shapes, patterns, words, doodles, and other connections of all kinds. This type of **Graphic Connector** makes your thinking visible. Some students find schoolwork easier when they can "see it."

You can use a **Mind Map** for almost any topic and have fun developing your own unique style for each one. Writing words in the JumpStart Box sparks creativity. Revisiting your Word Wall is another great place to start.

Mind Maps

Let's do it by the numbers. All you need to create a Mind Map is a topic, a few colored pencils, and a Mind Map template.

1. Begin your Mind Map with a symbol or picture representing an interesting topic.

2. Write key words (information rich nuggets) in the jump start box.

3. Arrange these words on your map in ways that makes sense to you.

4. Connect these words with lines showing how one key word relates to another.

5. Use color, picture, symbol, and codes to emphasize the relatedness of each group of words.

As your Mind Map evolves, its meaning will become increasingly obvious. When you use a Mind Map you will find that thinking, working, and problem solving become a lot more meaningful and fun.

Every Mind Map is different. By nurturing your individual self-expression, you are making a picture of your thinking.

The beauty of a Mind Map is that it is an easy-to-use comprehension strategy. As the image evolves, new ideas pop into your head.

A MindMap creates pictures of what you know using shapes, patterns, words, doodles, connections of all kinds. This type of Graphic Connector helps to make your thinking more visible so that you can relate to your studies in different ways. Write words in the JumpStart box to spark your creativity.

MIND MAP

Phases of Mitosis (animal cells)

G2 of Interphase
- 2 centrosomes form
- each centrosome has 2 centrioles

Metaphase
- Nucleus has disappeared
- chromosomes move toward the center of the cell & line up 46 chromosomes/92 chromatids

Telophase
- each set of chromosomes gets nuclear membrane & nuclei
- Microtubules dissolve

Prophase
- chromosomes become visible
- nuclear membrane disintegrates
- Centrosomes pull away from each other

Anaphase
- chromosomes separate at their centers
- chromatids move to opposite poles
- chromatids are referred to as daughter chromosomes

JUMP START

G2 of Interphase
Prophase
Metaphase
Anaphase
Cytokinesis

Nucleus
daughter chromosomes
nuclear membrane
centrosomes
chromosomes
centrioles

Nucleolus
chromatids
microtubules
daughter cells

MIND MAP

JUMP START

More Graphic Organizers

You won't use all of these for every assignment. Choose one or two that fit the lesson or assignment best.

Graphic Connectors:

- Select the organizer you think fits with what you are trying to study
- Draw the organizer in the space provided
- Fill in the appropriate information
- Tell a friend, teacher, or parent about your design

This Attribute Web describes the topic (in the middle) in five different ways.

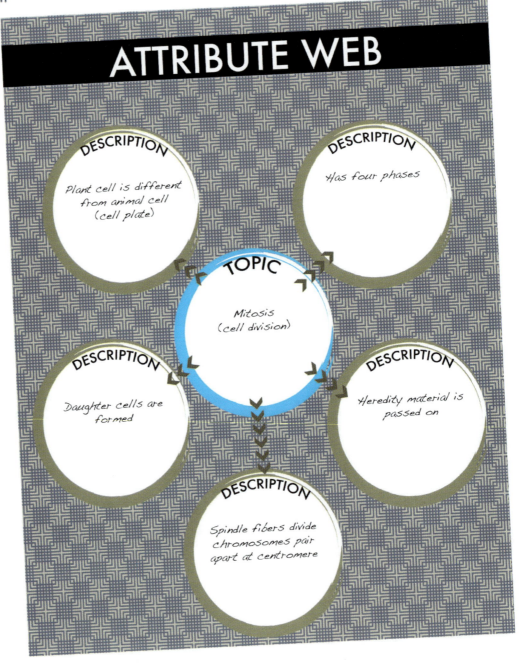

ATTRIBUTE WEB

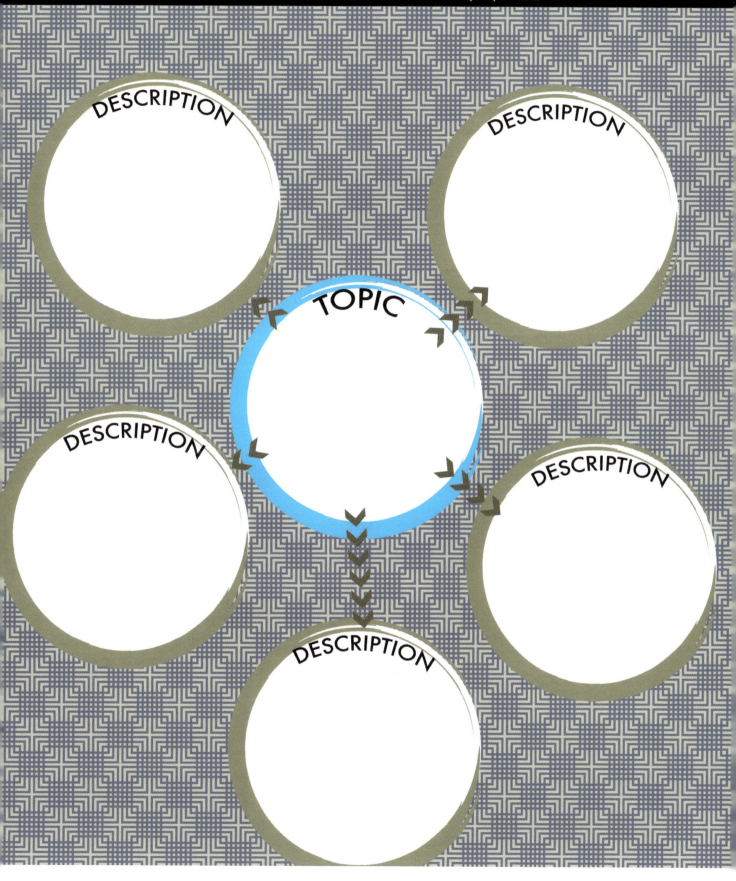

Many times you need to connect what you are studying with something else by finding out what they have in common. Here's your perfect opportunity to use a **Similarities Connector.**

SIMILARITIES

Animal Cell | Plant Cell

During prophase of both animal cells and plant cells, the chromatin condense and nucleoli begin to disappear.

The Mitotic process in animal cells and plant cells both contain 4 phases plus cytokinesis. They have the same end result.

During anaphase of both, chromatids of each chromosome have separated, and the daughter chromosomes are moving to the ends of the cell.

Sometimes you'll need to focus on qualities that make one thing **DIFFERENT** from another. The **Differences Connector** will really help you to "zero in" on exact definitions, formulas and distinguishing characteristics.

DIFFERENCES

Mitotic Division/Animal cells

In animals, growth takes place all over the animal's body until it reaches full size. Skin cells still retain the ability to grow.

During cytokinesis in animal cells, a cleavage furrow, a shallow groove in the cell surface near the old metaphase plate separates the two daughter cells.

Animal cells only have a cell membrane that protects them from outsides substances.

Mitotic Division/Plant cells

In plants, growth occurs in specialized areas called merisistems, which are in the root tip. Cell divisions increases in lenght.

During cytokinesis in plant cells, a cell plate separates the two daughter cells. The cell plate is made from vesicles from the Golgi that move along microtubules to the center.

Plant cells, not only have a cell membrane, but they also have a cell wall made of cellulose fibers.

DIFFERENCES

You might find a **Flow Chart** especially helpful when studying procedures or operations in math, science, or computer classes. Notice that the **Flow Chart** below follows a step-by-step format.

FLOW CHART

TOPIC: The Cell cycle

G₁ Phase

Cell grows
(Interphase)

S Phase
(DNA Synthesis)

Continues to grow copies chromosomes

G2 Phase

grows more as it prepares for division

M Phase

shortest part includes mitosis and cytoklhesis
(Mitotic phase)

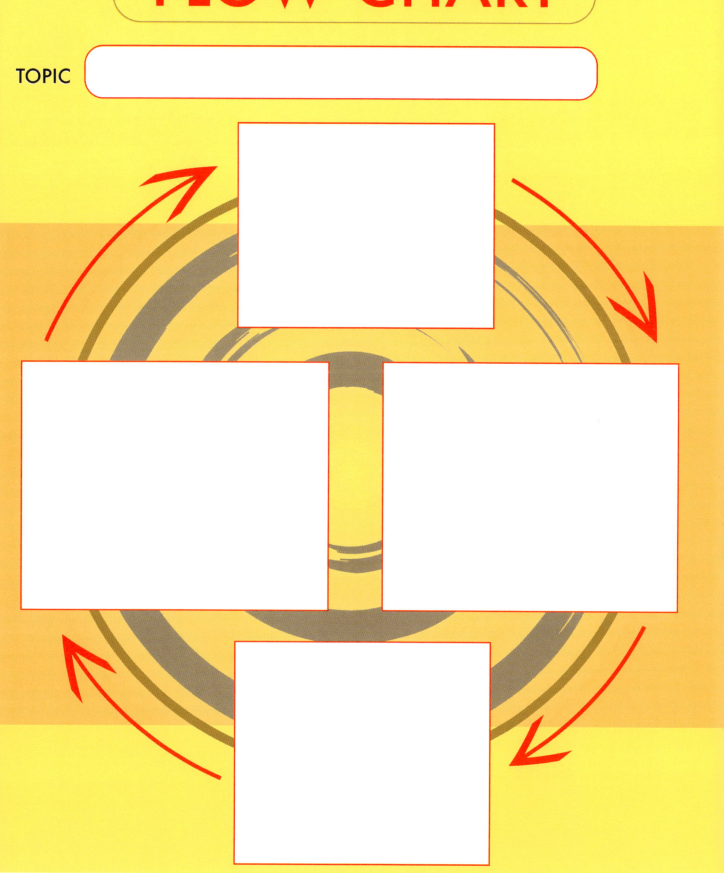

Whenever you are trying to remember key dates, the order of historical events, or happenings in your text or a story or film, try making a **TimeLine**. It's a great way to organize what comes first, next, then, and finally, as you see in this **TimeLine** on Mitosis. By the way, those four words are called (Can you remember?) . . . signal words.

TIME LINE

TOPIC: Mitosis: Plant Cell

FIRST
Prophase: chromatin is condensing; nucleus begins to disappear; mitotic spindle is starting to form.

NEXT
Metaphase: chromosomes become noticeable; each consist of two identical sister chromatids; nuclear envelope will fragment.

THEN
Anaphase: chromatids of each chromosome have separated, and daughter chromosomes move to ends of cell as their kinetochores microtubules shorten.

FINALLY
Telophase: daughter nuclei form; cytoplasm begins to divide

cytokinesis: the cell plate, which will divide the cytoplasm, is growing toward the outside.

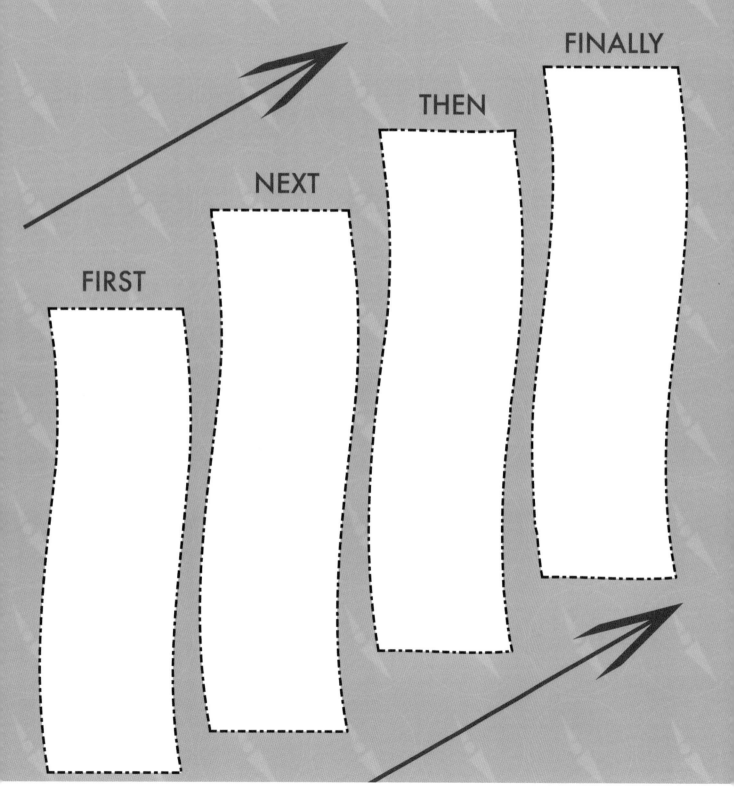

If You're Still Having Trouble, Try This!

1. Verbal and Visual Associations

To CONNECT and understand something new, change what you have read or heard to images, and what you have seen to words.

- If the new information comes in the form of words (either read or heard), try to form mental images or make a diagram of what you picture.
- If the new information comes in the form of a visual, think of the words to describe it to someone who hasn't seen it.

2. Simple Questions

- Sometimes, by asking ourselves simple questions, we make life-long connections. When CONNECTING, ask yourself:
    - What does this information remind me of?
    - How does this information fit with what I already know?
    - How am I going to remember this?

Lessons Learned

Connecting is that place in the learning cycle when the "light" in your brain comes on.

In the Connecting MindFrame, you experienced how learning makes better sense when ideas are linked together in meaningful ways.

You also learned that the graphic organizers you created to highlight similarities are actually high priority packaging labels. They send selected information to the place in your brain that holds knowledge for later use, for future learning, or for recall on a test.

Without proper categories for storage, new learning quickly becomes unmanageable. You should think of the Connecting MindFrame as your brain's "save all" function key. The Connecting MindFrame stores important information in a place that will be available as long as you need it.

Connecting is yet another learning strategy that adds to our motto: **Smart Is Self-Taught!**

In Your Own Words

Connecting strategies can help me become a more self-directed learner because…

To connect what I am learning, I will:

1. _____

2. _____

3. _____

4. _____

Coming Next

Recapping

Some things are more difficult to learn than others. For each person that differs, of course.

Recognizing what you know and deciding if you are prepared for new learning challenges is yet another characteristic of self-directed learning.

Experts call this learning behavior "self-monitoring" and it is by far one of the most important aspects of meaningful learning. StudyWhiz calls it RECAPPING.

Recapping is that place in the learning cycle where you—the learner—will stop for an "in progress" check on how things are going. Using the Recapping templates, you will learn to identify what you know and what you still need to learn. You will also recognize an important difference between need-to-know and nice-to-know information.

Can you rename the MindFrames up to this point?

P_____   N_____   C_____

MindFrame 4 is all about Recapping.

MindFrame: Recapping

Big Idea: Meaningful Learning Happens in Stages

IntroView

Who doesn't like TV?!

An average teenager, your age, daily spends nearly 6 1/2 hours with some sort of media—almost 4 hours of that time in front of a TV!

Top that off with your busy schedule and fast-paced life and you are bound to miss an episode of your favorite show. The media world knows this. That's why so many shows RECAP the last episode. Do you have any idea what the word "recap" means?

Most people love reality shows. Let's say you watch a particular show on a weekly basis. Later you talk to your friends about what happened that was hilarious or mind-boggling! One friend said she missed the whole show and wants to find out what happened. So you update your friend by recapping the episode.

Your recap helps your friend prepare herself for the next show without a "gap."

In the same regard, RECAPPING what you have learned in class makes future learning success more likely. While another can recap for you, unless you've been gone it's better to recap for yourself.

The most disastrous thing you can do is to take on new learning challenges with a serious "gap" in your understanding of previously covered material.

That is how students fall hopelessly behind in their studies. That is sad, since this problem could easily be avoided simply by spending a little quality time RECAPPING.

How Do You Stack Up Right Now as a Self-directed Learner Who Knows How to Recap?

Recapping: I keep track of what I already know and what I need to learn.

1. I make a list of what I know now and what I still need to know.
   - ☐ Never
   - ☐ Sometimes
   - ☐ Often

2. I remind myself that clearing up confusion is an important step to learning success.
   - ☐ Never
   - ☐ Sometimes
   - ☐ Often

3. I use my accomplishments to generate energy for future learning challenges.
   - ☐ Never
   - ☐ Sometimes
   - ☐ Often

4. I ask for help from my friends and teachers when I don't understand something.
   - ☐ Never
   - ☐ Sometimes
   - ☐ Often

Did You Know?

Have you ever heard the saying, "Use it, or lose it?" Most people have. But deep inside they are more than likely asking, "Use *what?*" Or, "Lose *what?*"

You have learned that your brain takes in information from your senses and the world around you. But how does your brain act on that information and send out messages to the rest of your body? How do you "use it" and not "lose it?"

Maybe you've heard the word metacognition.

Metacognition means thinking about thinking. Metacognition is our ability to know what we know and what we don't know. Study-Whiz calls this RECAPPING.

Recapping is checking your ability to produce evidence that you understand previously covered information. It is your ability to be conscious of your own learning and to reflect on and evaluate the quality of your thinking.

Believe it or not, RECAPPING is also re-learning. Whenever you test and consolidate your understanding of something you have learned, you re-learn it in more complete ways.

This is why explaining what you know to another student is a great strategy for deepening your own understanding of the topic. Try it!

It is true that the more you learn and retain, the more you can learn. Your brain gets in the habit of learning—and wants to learn more. Making more associations expands the brain's ability to retain information. With each new insight your human brain develops another set of branches (called dendrites) to which learning can be attached.
Even in your dreams you are actively trying to make sense of your life. Therefore, when you learn, pay attention to where you started, where you are now, and where you are going.

Recapping helps you know how far you have traveled in your learning and how much is left to go. That way you can fill in any gaps and get on to the goal!

Even after a lesson, it's smart to think about, review, and mentally play with your newly acquired knowledge. By recapping, you are literally doublingback on your learning to make sure you have covered all of the bases before taking on new challenges. When you see how much you have learned, your brain smiles.

And there's nothing better for a student than to have a happy brain!

Show You Know

The connections you make as you learn need to stand up to close observation—your own, first of all.

During **RECAPPING** your brain actually doubles back on itself and asks: *How well do I understand this new material? Well enough to move on? Or do I need to review a bit first?*

The first of the three templates you'll be using to **RECAP** is the 80-20 diagram.

> **The 80-20 Rule**
>
> Research tells us that 80% of what you need to learn is contained in 20% of the material you study. This secret is known as the "80-20 Rule."

This rule suggests that you are probably studying **TOO MUCH** stuff! (That's good news!) You can study less material and make better grades if you just **study smart!**

To create such a diagram, your mind needs to prioritize by asking:

What are the most and least important ideas in this lesson?

What's probably going to be on a quiz or test?

What will most likely form the best foundation for my future learning?

Recapping In Action

What you decide is most and least important can be gathered from the work you have already done with the other **MindFrames**, such as your **SmartNotes**, your **MindMaps, Webs,** etc.

Use this exercise as a review so you can fill in the second **RECAP** template, the **Know Chart** boxes on the following page. Your **Know Chart** makes your present study status visible to you. Jot down what you're quite sure of and what you might need to revisit before proceeding on with your lesson.

The Recap Rubric

Many learners do not have the courage to ask for help when learning stalls. (See the Recap page for an easy way to tell your teacher where you are in the learning process).

Although it is important to get immediate support, they prefer to hide the fact that they "simply don't get it." The Recap Rubric is one way to clarify the severity of the learning problem so the student can get help.

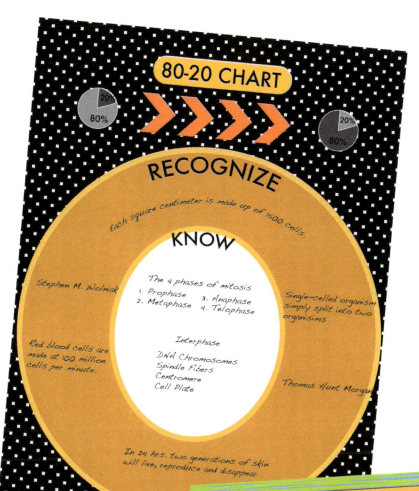

KNOW CHART

I KNOW

I NEED TO STUDY

RECAP RUBRIC

NAME: _____

CHAPTER TITLE: _____

DIRECTIONS: CHECK THE STATEMENT THAT BEST DESCRIBES YOUR COMFORT WITH WHAT YOU ARE LEARNING.

1 ☐ → → →

THIS INFORMATION IS STILL VERY CONFUSING TO ME

2 ☐ → → →

THIS INFORMATION MAKES SENSE TO ME, BUT I STILL MAKE SEVERAL MISTAKES WHEN I TRY TO DEMONSTRATE WHAT I KNOW

3 ☐ → → →

I UNDERSTAND THIS MATERIAL, BUT I STILL MAKE A FEW MISTAKES WHEN I TRY TO DEMONSTRATE WHAT I KNOW.

4 ☐ → → →

I UNDERSTAND THIS MATERIAL AND I AM READY FOR NEW CHALLENGES

If You Are Having Trouble, Try This!

When recapping, you might do better if you shut out sensory input, i.e., turn off the TV, move to a quiet room, put away distractions like cell phones, don't eat and drink, etc. That way your brain is not receiving new sensory information at the same time it is working with old.

- **Getting it**
  Are you feeling overwhelmed or like you just don't "get" it? You probably get a lot more than you think (or give yourself credit for), but a few points are throwing you for a loop. Try scoring your level of comprehension on a scale of 1 to 10. (1 = no understanding; 10 = complete understanding)

Retrace your learning steps by scanning the text and scoring each section. This will help you see just how much you do understand and where you need to revisit and refocus your attention.

- **Finding the missing piece of the puzzle**
  Look at each of your Word Wall words. Can you explain the significance of a word as it relates to the text or the class lecture? Try doing this with a study buddy, so you can help fill in the missing gaps in each other's learning. Plus, explaining what you've learned to others cements those thoughts in long-term memory. If you both are stuck on a word, ask another peer or your teacher for clarity.

Lessons Learned

In this chapter on RECAPPING you learned that your mind RE-LEARNS new material when it RECAPS. It doubles back and looks over everything one more time before moving forward. Recapping is rehearsing and repeating newly learned information in ways that affirm understanding.

At this point in the learning cycle, self-directed learners have set the stage for meaningful learning by directing their attention to aspects of the information that are particularly important (PREVIEWING).

Then they use names of important concepts, events, people, and terms to generate notes about important characteristics they will need to know (NAMING).

After that they group these important ideas in ways that make understanding and remembering easier (CONNECTING).

And, finally, they double back over what they have learned to guarantee that they are satisfied with their understanding of the material. (RECAPPING).

In Your Own Words

RECAPPING strategies can help me become a more self-directed learner because…

To recap, I will:

1. _____
2. _____
3. _____
4. _____

Coming Next

Constructing

The next MindFrame, **CONSTRUCTING**, is where you'll find the action!

When your mind constructs, it demonstrates that you can use what you are learning in many different ways.

Constructing is when students use learning to do the work of writers, authors, scientists, mathematicians and artists. It is when learners test and consolidate learning in ways that deepen meaning and understanding.

In the Constructing MindFrame, students also create Study Briefs that serve as snapshots of what they need to know. Study Briefs are information-packed "chunks" that can be used for sharing and deepening understanding. (Check out the StudyBriefs in your PREVIEW of the next chapter.)

In Constructing, students also write about and share how they feel about the learning experiences.

MindFrame 5 is all about Constructing—the action step!

MindFrame: Constructing

Big Idea: Constructing is Taking Learning Beyond the Textbook—to Make it Your Own

IntroView

Writing is yet another way to become a more self-directed learner. By struggling with facts and organizing information into a form that can be communicated to someone else, students sharpen their thinking skills.

In short, if students are to learn in meaningful ways, they must write.

As a teen, you write a lot. You may not have noticed it, but your life is filled with writing. Let's look at some of the ways you write. First, there's the **formal writing** you do in school: term papers, essays, project reports, notes, journals, learning logs, test responses, study guides, etc.

Secondly, there is the **non-school writing** that teens do for personal enjoyment. Most teens say that they enjoy writing to friends via MySpace, Face Book, e-mail, and text or instant messaging.

Even though electronic writing is different from formal writing, it is a form of expression that involves thinking and communicating ideas.

So it counts!

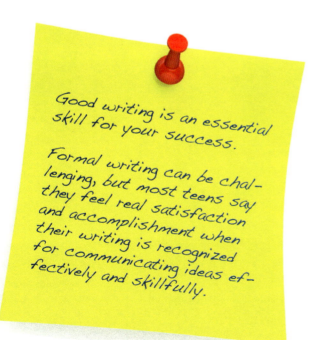

Good writing is an essential skill for your success.

Formal writing can be challenging, but most teens say they feel real satisfaction and accomplishment when their writing is recognized for communicating ideas effectively and skillfully.

No matter what types of writing you do, all of it has one element in common—you must CONSTRUCT what you are writing.

Whether writing a research report or an instant message, think "sandwich."

All sandwich recipes are the same: something between two slices of bread. (Do you prefer peanut butter, or jelly? Maybe both!)

The same is true with writing. Whether you're writing a research report or an instant message, you will always have the same basic "ingredients": an introduction, the body, and a conclusion.

Put them together and you have written communication. You knew something and you put it down on paper. In other words, you CONSTRUCTED, so that someone else could read what you know.

That's exactly how your mind frames new material. Your mind **CONSTRUCTS** what it is learning to achieve a further goal.

Learning usually begins by taking things in, but sooner or later it shifts to putting things out. You will remember and use what you learn better by creating evidence of what you know. To do that you need to construct.

A construction site is a place with lots of action, and this **CONSTRUCTING** MindFrame is where the action is!

When your mind constructs, it demonstrates that you can use what you are learning.

You **CONSTRUCT** when you figure out the answers to questions at the end of a chapter, when you explain your ideas, or give a solution to a problem.

You are also **CONSTRUCTING** when you design a project, conduct a science experiment, or build a web site.

CONSTRUCTING happens easily when you become curious about how something works. It's your mind's way of "shifting gears" to solve new problems.

CONSTRUCTING is also the strategy the mind uses to put things together in ways that make sense and that can be used. When CONSTRUCTING, your mind develops deeper levels of understanding and stores the information in memory.

"Use it or lose it" is especially true when it comes to your schoolwork. Can you see how important the constructing component is to remembering information?

How Do You Stack Up Right Now as a Self-directed Learner Who Knows How to Construct?

Constructing: Taking learning beyond the textbook to make it your own.

1. I seek opportunities to test my ability by expressing and communicating what I know in different ways.

☐ Never ☐ Sometimes ☐ Often

2. I challenge myself to write about what I am learning in order to deepen my understanding.

☐ Never ☐ Sometimes ☐ Often

3. I work with classmates to create & complete projects or products that provide evidence of our learning-in-action.

☐ Never ☐ Sometimes ☐ Often

4. I create study materials that prepare me for unit tests and classroom evaluations of progress.

☐ Never ☐ Sometimes ☐ Often

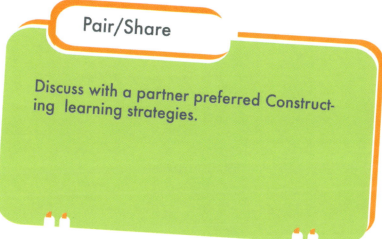

Pair/Share

Discuss with a partner preferred Constructing learning strategies.

Did you know?

Even though a computer can receive information on its own, it needs software to interpret the data.

Your brain is similar. While receiving information, it needs something else to process the information. Your brain must engage its own "software."

A computer, even with the right software, cannot retain information without saving it. Your brain needs to link what it is being taught with what you already know. You might need to test the learning, recap it, or even explain it to yourself or someone else in order to "save" the information in your memory banks. That is all part of constructing.

Ask yourself questions like:

- Have I heard or seen this information before?
- What does it remind me of?
- Where does this information fit?
- What can I do with it?
- What does it mean?

Show You Know

StudyBriefs

StudyBriefs are like note cards that help students summarize, organize, and consolidate information they will need to remember for a test. The cards help students monitor their understanding by creating a format for them to extend or clarify their thinking.

Experts tell us that successful students create personalized methods for getting good grades. Such methods allow them to **study hard** when it is time to study and **play hard** when it is time to play!

These students are not more intelligent than other students. They just know how to get the most out of the time they spend on schoolwork. They study *smart!*

> In a special study of successful students, all prepared for major tests or projects in similar ways:
>
> *First*, they created note cards for different categories of information, such as important people, key ideas, historical events, timelines, definitions and rules.
>
> *Second*, they detailed each note card with a title, definition(s), facts, a page reference, and a personal note to help with remembering the information.
>
> *Third*, they personalized the note cards with doodled symbols for interest and fun.
>
> And, *finally*, the students organized these cards to create a storyline that could be extended and remembered.

Later, the storyline could be transformed into an essay. If you can write an essay that even your friends can understand, you can be sure your learning is on the right track.

StudyWhiz calls these note cards **StudyBriefs**. **StudyBriefs** enable you to quickly make study prompts that will improve your memory and understanding. They are handy snapshots of important information you need to study.

If you can make a **StudyBrief** without a problem, then you know the material. If you cannot fill in each section of the **StudyBrief**, you have gaps in your knowledge about that subject.

Each **StudyBrief** is a power pack of important information—or what's commonly called a **"chunk."** **Chunking** is great stuff for learners because each time you make a good **StudyBrief**, you practice thinking in an organized way.

By using information from your other **MindFrames**, you can easily create **StudyBriefs** that will help you to complete homework assignments, write class essays, give speeches, complete projects, study for tests, and *shine* in classroom discussions.

Here are the four different kinds of StudyBriefs: (1) Terms/ Concepts, (2) People, (3) Events, and (4) Other.

StudyBriefs

Terms/ Concepts: Key ideas, important concepts, terms, points of emphasis from your books, and notes.

People: This will be particularly useful in language arts, social studies, and science-subjects where you're learning about people in history and scientific advancements, plus characters in literature.

Events: Think of major happenings when you work on your **Events StudyBrief.** Include information such as action (plot) in stories, historical events and significant scientific, mathematical and technological occurrences.

Other: Most of what you study should fit into one of the previous three **StudyBrief** categories: Terms, People, Events. However, when you come upon something that doesn't seem to fit, make an **Other StudyBrief.** Your "other" section might even be the most interesting!

Learning is natural, pleasurable, spontaneous to the brain. If that is not true, something is wrong.
—Richard Restak

STUDYBRIEF

- ☑ Terms/ Concepts
- ☐ People
- ☐ Events
- ☐ Other

CONTACT POINT

Mitosis

DOODLE BOX

1. Prophase

2. Metaphase

3. Anaphase

4. Telophase

REFERENCE IN TEXT

Page 46-50

IN YOUR OWN WORDS

Mitosis is the division of cells and takes place in four phases - prophase, metaphase, anaphase and telophase.

FORMAL DEFINITION

The type of cell division by which two daughter cells are formed.

SUPPORTING FACTS / EXAMPLES

The nucleus breaks.
The chromosomes twist and thicken. Spindle fibers attach to the centromere and pull the chromosomes apart. They move to each end and the cell divides.

SAMPLE TEST QUESTIONS

What is mitosis?
Name the 4 phases of mitosis
What is interphase?
What is the difference between animal and plant mitosis?

StudyBrief

○ Terms/ Concepts
○ People
○ Events
○ Other

CONTACT POINT

DOODLE BOX

REFERENCE IN TEXT

IN YOUR OWN WORDS

FORMAL DEFINITION

SUPPORTING FACTS / EXAMPLES

SAMPLE TEST QUESTIONS

If You Are Having Trouble, Try This!

Check Your Channel ... Is it on?

Dr. Mel Levine, an expert on memory and learning, talks about the different "channels" we have in our brains—and how we should make sure to be "tuned" to the right channel when attempting a difficult task.

Sometimes students assume a task is too hard, when, in fact, they are just tuned to the wrong channel. It's not uncommon to sometimes be "off channel." What is important is to figure out that we are.

Your ability to CONSTRUCT might be hampered if you are not in the right frame of mind—the "constructing" channel. Ask yourself these 3 questions to be sure you're ready to CONSTRUCT:

(1) Have I chosen a place to work where I can give my full concentration to the task at hand?
(2) Have I set aside enough time to give this task the attention it deserves and needs?
(3) Have I cleared my mind of issues—**and tuned to the "constructing" channel?**

Make it Real!

Make sure you have deepened and extended your thinking beyond the two covers of the textbook and the four walls of the classroom. There is more than one level of comprehension. Self-directed learners want to make the learning their own!

Study these three levels of comprehension. Understanding the differences between "literal" and "inference" and "relevant" comprehension are important even before you CONSTRUCT.

> **Literal Level:** "What did the text or teacher say?"
> (on the surface, restating)
>
> **Inference Level:** "What did it (what you read or heard) mean?"
> (evidence from text, where your thoughts are revealed)
>
> **Relevant Level:** "Why does it (what you have learned) matter?"
> (its impact on you/your peers, your family/the world/society today; the connection to the human condition)

Metaphoric Thoughts ... Think outside the box!

Often, constructing a metaphor helps to connect your new learning to the world. A metaphor is a shortcut to the meaning. It sets two unlike things side by side and makes us see the likeness between them. It also creates a picture in your mind.

For example: "After StudyWhiz, preparing for a test is a walk in the park."

What does that mean? What would it mean to write, "Preparing for a test used to be a steep climb against the wind"?

Another famous metaphor is, *"All the world's a stage"* (Shakespeare). What does that mean?

Of course, the phrase THINK OUTSIDE THE BOX is also a metaphor! Can you think of others?

Lessons Learned

In this chapter on **CONSTRUCTING**, you learned that the more connections you can make between what you know and what you are learning, the more likely you are to understand and remember.

Experts tell us that the best connections are made by experimenting with what works in the real world. You can solve problems, summarize and re-state what you know, and, in the end you should formulate new questions based on a change in your understanding.

You have also learned that writing is a reliable test of your ability to give structure and meaning to your newly discovered understandings.

In Your Own Words

Constructing strategies can help me become a more self-directed learner because...

To construct what I am learning, I will:

1. _____

2. _____

3. _____

4. _____

Coming Next:
Self-Testing

Congratulations! You are now in the final phase of learning how to become a self-directed learner.

In MindFrame one you learned about the importance of checking out how much you already know about a new subject and directing your attention to what is important in this new content. This is PREVIEWING.

You then moved to taking SMART NOTES that help you define the meaning of new concepts and add facts and related information to these definitions so that you can organize your thinking and make sense of this new information. This is NAMING.

Once you collected enough new information, you began to chunk and sort what you were learning into categories using GRAPHIC ORGANIZERS that would make remembering this information easier. This is CONNECTING.

At that point in the learning cycle, you stopped to assess how much you really understood and re-learn important information that you were not confident about. Here, taking on more information would not be smart. This is RECAPPING.

And, finally, you reached the point in the learning cycle where you are ready to use what you have learned by experimenting with it, demonstrating you understood it, writing about what others have done with it, defending your opinions about its importance, and even creating new ways to think about it. This is CONSTRUCTING.

The next step on your journey to becoming a self-directed learner is called SELF-TESTING. Self-Testing is where you show how well you understand these new ideas!

The Self-Testing MindFrame is important because it will take the fear out of testing! (Preview this next chapter quickly so you can get to the content. You'll love it.)

MindFrame: Self-Testing

Big Idea: Self-testing Will Ease Fears Before a Test—and Make You Proud After the Test

IntroView

Think about the last time you were at a sporting event or some other competition with one of your rival schools. Before the competition, your school may have had a pep rally. The band played the school song. Your school's name was announced and participants' names were shouted out in an enthusiastic voice booming out from a microphone.

Way before that moment came hours and hours–if not weeks and months–of practice and rehearsal. And during those final rehearsals, all the event participants were SELF-TESTING to determine their readiness for the performance or game.

It's like target practice—seeing how close you can get to the bull's-eye!

Learning also involves rehearsing. It usually starts by asking yourself questions similar to these:

- What have I learned?
- What do I need to understand more deeply?
- What do I now believe?
- What are my skills?
- What do I need to improve?

Taking time for self-testing gives you the opportunity to examine and highlight what you know **now** that you may not have known **before**.

How Do You Stack Up As A Self-directed Learner Who Knows How To Self-test?

Self-Testing: I prepare for tests in advance by testing myself.

1. I write challenging questions and practice getting them correct.

☐ Never   ☐ Sometimes   ☐ Often

2. I create talking points and read them aloud to hear myself learning.

☐ Never   ☐ Sometimes   ☐ Often

3. I test myself using personally constructed study briefs.

☐ Never   ☐ Sometimes   ☐ Often

4. I ask my classmates and my teachers to give me feedback on my understanding before the test.

☐ Never   ☐ Sometimes   ☐ Often

Pair/Share

Discuss with a partner the most reliable Self-Testing strategies.

Did You Know?

Are you aware that **learning** and **retention** (remembering) are very different? You can learn something and in just a few minutes forget it. (Some students do that when they "cram" before a test.)

Retention is that process where the important things you learn are stored in your brain and preserved for future use. In school, retention matters!

Retention is influenced by many things, but none as important as **rehearsal. Rehearsal is what you do to help yourself remember important information for a test.**

StudyWhiz calls this **SELF-TESTING. Rehearsal and self-testing are the same.**

There are many forms of Self-Testing. You have to find those that work best for you. Here are some ideas:

(1) Reading your notes out loud and then quizzing yourself.
(2) Writing an essay about an important topic to see how much you know.
(3) Making note cards and arranging them in an order that you can use to tell a story about what you know.
(4) Telling what you have learned to your friends, your family–even your dog! (This out loud speaking helps your brain store new learning in a place where it can be retrieved in the future.)
(5) Using your Smart Notes.

Whether you make your own practice test or quiz out loud with friends, your ability to use what you learn in the future will be greatly improved the more you self-test.

Hold on, now. Get *ready* now for some big terminology: Primacy-Recency Effect.

Can you guess what that phrase means? Look at the middle word recency. I'm sure you'll recognize that as a form of "recent." Any guesses now?

> Here's the explanation of **Primacy-Recency Effect:**
>
> When you are learning, you will remember best what you learned first.
> **Learned First = Remembered BEST.**
>
> You will remember second best what you learned last.
> **Learned Last = Remembered SECOND Best**
>
> And, you guessed it; your brain will remember **least** what came just past the middle.
> **Middle = You'll be lucky to remember this at all!**

Does this theory make sense to you? Why or why not?

The first (new) information gets your attention and goes to the semantic (memory) portion of your brain. The middle information tends to exceed the capacity of the working memory and can get lost. (StudyWhiz techniques will help you retain the middle information better, however.)

As the learning concludes, items in your working memory are sorted or "chunked" to allow for additional processing of the last few items. These will probably be held in working memory—but might decay unless further rehearsed. (This all comes from research by Gazzanniga et al., 2002; Terry, 2005).

Practice does not make perfect—because you might be practicing all the wrong things. Has that ever happened to you?

Practice does, however, make things permanent. And the right kind of practice will make you a better student!

Practice in the form of **Self-Testing** will provide real evidence that you know what you think you know. And when it comes to doing well on classroom testing, the confidence you get from Self-Testing is worth its weight in gold.

When your mind successfully **Self-Tests**, it sends the signal that *the coast* is clear to take on new challenges. This signal is an essential part of the learning process.

Before **Self-directed Learners** take any form of test or enter a competition, they **SELF-TEST:** They go over the material one final time—like a play's dress rehearsal or a final practice in football.

If you were about to enter a writing contest, here's an example of what you *might* do in the self-testing segment. (You could substitute science fair here—or speech or music competition.)

In this case, that real event is the judging of your essay by a panel of computer researchers. They are coming to a nearby civic center to make their selection from all 20 schools that have entered the contest.

Before you turn in your class essay, you set up a mock judges' panel to evaluate the essay for accuracy, clarity and creativity. You test the essay under "fire," adjust it where necessary, and submit it.

Again, a smart self-taught learner fully prepares for what comes next by self-testing! And you don't have to **SELF-TEST** alone. You can do it with your friends and classmates. After all, you'll all be there together on the big day.

That's exactly how your mind frames new material when it **SELF-TESTS.** It gives you a warm-up, a dress rehearsal for whatever test awaits.

The **Self-Testing MindFrame** is so important. If you practice enough by testing yourself, the tests from your teacher won't seem as threatening.

Good teachers should prepare students for tests and should celebrate their accomplishments. But in case that doesn't always happen, **prepare** and **celebrate** yourself!

You can actually use all your **MindFrames** for **Self-Testing.** In fact, you can probably even invent creative ways of using each template to make tests and reviews for yourself and your friends.

For example, you might arrange your **StudyBriefs** in an order that makes sense to you. (Your order may be different from everyone else's and that's just fine.) The way you arrange your **StudyBriefs** will be your way of remembering the information.

Several StudyWhiz templates are designed just for the Self-Test **MindFrame**. The first one, the **Know Chart,** will look familiar because you used it already to **RECAP**.

The second, **Talking Points**, will give you a chance to rehearse out loud before you take the test.

Use your **Know Chart** the same way you did in the **RECAPPING MindFrame.** This time, however, you probably know more material and have fewer items in your **Need-to-Study** box.

When learning, the more senses you use the better. **Talking Points** will help you add the sound of your own voice to your other learning tools. Using three cards, jot down short phrases or key words that will help you tell a story about what you've learned.

As you talk it through, you may need to rearrange the order of your key ideas to make your story flow more naturally and make more sense. Practice telling your story **out loud** to a friend, a parent, or to yourself. All this builds memory power!

Show You Know

A great way to check your understanding of a topic is by folding the SmartNotes page to reveal only the Cue Words Column. Everything in this column should triger your memory and lead you to the more detailed information included in your notes.

If you are having trouble, try this!

Before Class

- Reread your notes (at least from the previous day and any homework) to set the stage for new connections you make

During Class

- Continue to develop new pages of SmartNotes
- Listen for important ideas
- Jot down phrases and key words as possible Cue Words
- Underline, circle, and use your coding symbols
- Use abbreviations
- Translate. Do NOT write down every word you hear
- Record and highlight any suggested test questions
- Put down page numbers from your text where more info can be found

After Class

- Make sure you have filled in the topic and date
- Complete the Cue Words Column
- Add any new material from reading or class discussion to Notes Column
- Use SmartNotes to make Graphic Connectors when appropriate

Lessons Learned

In this chapter on Self-Testing you were reminded that **learning is not the same thing as remembering.**

You also learned that Self-Testing (known as Rehearsal) is a **personal experience**. Some Self-Testing strategies are better than others, depending upon your learning style.

Self-directed Learners understand the importance of testing their own knowledge and ability before their teachers do.

Can't you imagine that Self-Testing might mean the difference between getting a "C" and an "A" on an important test?

In Your Own Words

Self-Testing strategies can help me become a more self-directed learner because…

A mind stretched to a new idea never goes back to its original dimensions.

—Oliver Wendell Holmes, jurist

To Self-Test what I am learning, I will:

1. _____

2. _____

3. _____

4. _____

Coming Next: **Reflecting**

The final MindFrame in the StudyWhiz process is **Reflecting**.

In the fast-paced life of a modern student, REFLECTING is often overlooked as a critical element in the learning process.

Our "just do it" lifestyle emphasizes action over reflection. But humans are hardwired to balance reflection and action when learning.

Reflection, when added to your decision that new information is important, plays a huge role in your natural learning system.

Without the "soak in" time that comes to the brain through Reflection, much of what you have learned will not be appropriately assessed for value – and therefore lost. What this means is that the learning cycle is not completed properly until the learner "doubles back" over what has been learned and sorts information into "**Need to Keep**" or "**Nice to Keep**" categories.

MindFrame 7 is all about Reflecting. Since this is so important, aren't you glad to know that what you learn last is remembered second best?

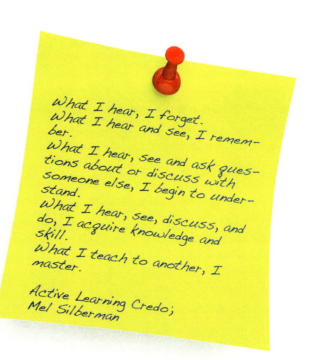

What I hear, I forget.
What I hear and see, I remember.
What I hear, see and ask questions about or discuss with someone else, I begin to understand.
What I hear, see, discuss, and do, I acquire knowledge and skill.
What I teach to another, I master.

Active Learning Credo;
Mel Silberman

MindFrame: Reflecting

Big Idea: Reflecting Puts Things in Perspective. It Leaves You Changed

IntroView

Meaning is so powerful that most states prohibit trial lawyers from using what is known as the "Golden Rule" argument. The Golden Rule argument is, **"If you were in that person's situation, what would you have done?"**

For example, if someone is breaking into your house and you shoot that person, you could face murder charges. At the trial, your attorney can't say to the jury, "If someone were breaking into your home, wouldn't you do the same?"

Why do you think the Golden Rule argument can't be used?

Learning is a journey. When you make connections to your past experiences, your current experience and your future learning become meaningful to you.

When you relate the learning to your needs, wants, interests, and values, the chance that meaning will be stored in your brain and used throughout your life increases immensely.

And when you know something well enough to share it with someone else almost effortlessly, you have mastered it. You "own" the knowledge. The journey has left you changed!

How Do You Stack Up As A Self-directed Learner Who Knows How To Reflect?

Reflecting: I make notes to myself about my learning experiences.

1. I record my feelings about what I enjoyed and what surprised me during a unit.
   ☐ Never   ☐ Sometimes   ☐ Often

2. I make personal notes about what I am really good at when it comes to learning.
   ☐ Never   ☐ Sometimes   ☐ Often

3. I make journal notes about how I may improve my learning ability in the future.
   ☐ Never   ☐ Sometimes   ☐ Often

4. I ask myself, "What new questions do I have about what I learned?"
   ☐ Never   ☐ Sometimes   ☐ Often

Pair/Share

Discuss with a partner your most reliable learning strategy.

Did You Know

Think these questions through and then share your experiences:

- Have you ever been so angry you nearly burst at the seams?
- Or so sad that the phrase "crying your heart out" made sense?
- Or so excited you couldn't help but scream?

Scientists break down emotions into six basic types: happiness, sadness, anger, surprise, disgust, and fear. You show each emotion by one of six specific facial expressions.

Making these faces is not something you "learned"; it's a part of all of us. Even people who are blind make these same faces when they are sad or mad or happy. Our emotions are who we are. They are internal, but are often displayed externally.

Your brain's "**limbic system**" is an amazing center of memory and emotion. In fact, it is even sometimes referred to as the "**emotional brain**" because this is where your emotions and memories are stored. The two parts of the limbic system are (1) the **hippocampus** and (2) the **amygdala**.

The *hippocampus* sorts through and controls how long and where your memories will be stored. It makes decisions about what's worth keeping in long-term memory. Compare it to a spaghetti strainer that separates the noodles (important facts and details) from the water (non-important facts and details).

The *amygdala* is the emotional center which interprets non-verbal information from your senses (images, sounds, smells, etc.) and decides how your body should react to an emotional situation. The amygdala is known to be responsible for your "fight or flight" response.

For example, have you ever thought something (a baseball, a bird, someone's fist, etc.) was going to hit you in the head so you ducked—only to find out it was a shadow instead? This was your amygdala taking over before your thinking brain (the cortex) could get involved and see the shadow.

Your amygdala wants to keep you safe. It compares the event or situation to previous memories and knowledge and then sends information to other parts of your brain on how to react.

It's important for you to know this: Two parts of your brain (the hippocampus and amygdala) team up to help you understand and deal with your feelings. They work together to help you connect your memories and emotions in meaningful ways so you can better understand the world. They connect past and new learning to your own life so that it matters to you! And they work together to internalize meaning, putting things into perspective. When all this happens, you are changed!

Now, how can you help your brain do these things at school? By reflecting! The word **REFLECT** means "to bend back." By adding your presonal reflections your learning becomes stronger and more memorable.

At the end of each major lesson or unit, the best **Self-Directers Learners** reflect or "bend back" to the beginning of their learning journey to get a sense of what has happened. They want to see (reflect) how they are growing as learners.

True learning is a deeply personal, deeply reflective experience. It engages you and begins your transformation into the person you will become.

Reflection begins with YOU. It's natural to ask yourself, "What does this text mean to *me*?" But in order for deep reflection to happen and leave you changed as a learner and as a person, you need to think of reflection in thoughts (or layers) beyond yourself.

Have you ever thrown a rock out into a lake? If so, you saw the "ripple effect." Explain what you think that means. (Draw a picture in your notebook.)

The ripples circle out into layers (rings) beyond the point of entry. This "ripple effect" is a picture of what happens when you reflect deeply and move beyond just information to how the text impacts you and your life.

John Powers created a model called "Circles of Reflection" that shows different levels, or layers, of reflection. Thinking of these layers can help you push beyond yourself and into deeper levels of reflection.

Think beyond yourself and ask, "What does this information in this text mean to my family? My friends and peers? My community? My country? To humankind?" These reflections will leave you permanently changed.

It's like an artist who added details to a picture. You are the artist—so your picture will be unique to you. As your growth happens, it is helpful to have some kind of record of your learning journey.

And now you do! The first six **MindFrames** in your **StudyWhiz** give you records of your thinking.

This final **MindFrame (REFLECTING)** offers you the opportunity to honor what you are feeling and realizing and questioning—at levels even deeper than yourself.

As part of your reflection, jot down your feelings about what you have studied:

- What things surprised you?
- What did you find interesting that you didn't know before?
- What tasks did you find difficult—and how did you deal with them?
- What activities did you do in the unit that helped you enjoy the learning more?

And the most important question:

 Why does this learning matter?

Show You Know

Here are two templates to encourage your reflection, a **Content Journal** and a **Personal Journal.** Turn the page to see examples of these powerful journals.

The **Content Journal** sticks more closely to the material you have learned and allows you one final opportunity to record what you found interesting and important, to draw and doodle some reminders, and to make a very general summary of the whole topic.

The **Personal Journal** provides space for you to reflect on yourself as a learner, on what this learning experience was like on the inside in terms of your feelings, reactions and insights.

CONTENT JOURNAL

SUMMARY NOTES

Interphase prepares the cell by storing extra energy and duplicating DNA. Mitosis then begins and occurs in 4 stages, prophase, metaphase, anaphase and telophase. After the cell divides, interphase occurs again and prepares for the process of mitosis to begin all over again.

Write a summary paragraph or story about what you learned.

PICTURES

1. Prophase

2. Metaphase

3. Anaphase

4. Telophase

Draw "doodle symbols" that remind you of what you need to know.

IMPORTANT

Prophase
Interphase
Metaphase
Anaphase
Telophase
DNA
Chromosomes
Centromere
Mitosis
Spindle fibers
Cell plates
Stephen Wolniak
Thomas Hunt Morgan

What ideas, terms, events, people, did your teacher emphasize?

INTERESTING

How the cell duplicates the hereditary material so that it can split off again and again.

Start Here

What was the most interesting thing you learned in this unit?

CONTENT JOURNAL

SUMMARY NOTES

Write a summary paragraph or story about what you learned.

PICTURES

Draw "doodle symbols" that remind you of what you need to know.

INTERESTING

What was the most interesting thing you learned in this unit?

Start Here

IMPORTANT

What ideas, terms, events, people, did your teacher emphasize?

PERSONAL JOURNAL

I recently learned that...

Cells divide by the process of mitosis. Mitosis occurs in four stages - prophase, metaphase, anaphase and telophase.

This is interesting to me because...

It is fascinating that the cell can contain and activate a process that keeps reproducing new cells in order to replace dying ones.

I wish I could...

See a video recording of the process of mitosis in action.

PERSONAL JOURNAL

I recently learned that...

This is interesting to me because...

I wish I could...

Here are some extra reflection-starters for your **Personal Journal** Template. You may want to use different ones at different times.

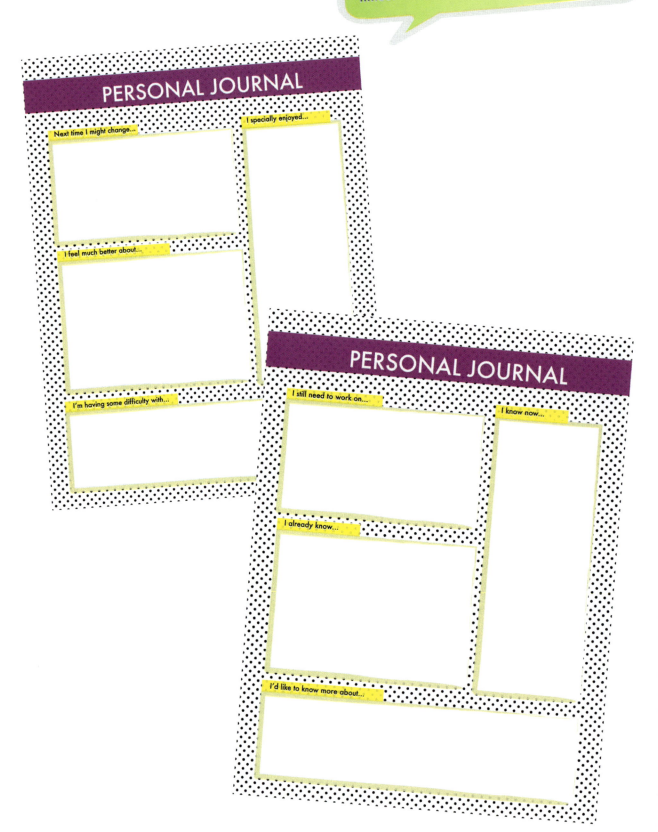

PERSONAL JOURNAL

Next time I might change…

I specially enjoyed…

I feel much better about…

I'm having some difficulty with…

PERSONAL JOURNAL

I still need to work on...

I know now...

I already know...

I'd like to know more about...

If you are having trouble, try this!

You've heard of "traveling back in time"?

Sometimes, thinking of your learning as a journey from a starting point to a destination helps you "travel back in time" in regards to how you have changed along the way. It prepares your thoughts for deeper reflection and journaling.

> Go back to the beginning of your learning journey:
>
> - Look through your Word Wall, SmartNotes, and graphic connectors.
> - Scan your StudyBriefs.
> - Then return to the "Circles of Reflection."

In the "Circles of Reflection," on page 126, start with the innermost circle (the self) and ask, "What does this learning mean to me? How does it impact my life?"

Then go to the next circle layer (the family) and ask: "What does this learning mean to my family? How does it impact them?"

Continue through the layers until you feel ready to journal.

Lessons Learned

In this chapter on REFLECTING you learned that true learning is deeply personal because it changes you. What this means is that learning is one way we can take control of our own destiny. By organizing how we think about and react to our experiences we can change ourselves from the inside out. The more we learn and the more complete our thinking becomes the more options we have.

Reflecting is how the human brain bends back and cleans up our thinking so that important information can be stored for future use. Without reflection, thinking and learning are less likely to survive long enough to get stored in our memory.

You have learned that self-directed learners make a record of how learning changed them. By taking advantage of this incredible learning power that is only possible during "down time"—(when we are not acting) learners greatly enhance their learning power.

In Your Own Words

Write a three paragraph essay defending or rejecting the following statement:

> Smart is the ability to think about my own thoughts in ways that help me make better decisions. Smart is my ability to reflect with purpose.

To REFLECT upon what I am learning I will:

1. _____

2. _____

3. _____

4. _____

SECTION 3

StudyWhiz Taxonomy

Project Guide: Create Your Own StudyWhiz System

The Study Whiz Taxonomy

The Study Whiz Taxonomy: How High Can You Go?

Directions: The following questions are arranged from easiest to most difficult. Question one is a knowledge question. Number two is a comprehension question. Number three is an application question. Number four is an analysis question. Number five is a synthesis question. And number six is an evaluation question. You should begin with number one and see how high you can go.

1. Knowledge: Create a mind map of the Seven MindFrames.

2. Comprehension: Explain how the seven MindFrames will help you succeed in school: Previewing helps me…

3. Application: Using the Smart Notes template, make a sample notes page using at least 4 concepts or terms in the cue column.

4. Analysis: Compare and contrast the learning behaviors of self-directed learners with students who are not self-directed.

5. Synthesis: Summarize how Study Whiz can help students improve their participation in classroom activities.

6. Evaluation: Read the following statement:
Students with the highest I.Q. have an easy time in school and always get the best grades. I agree/disagree with this statement because…

Project Guide: Create Your Own StudyWhiz System

What's Next?

You are now ready to use the StudyWhiz techniques.

If this were a movie, you'd be the director. If this were a band, you'd be the conductor. If this were a team, you'd be the coach.

You are in charge of your own learning and success in school. You are a self-directed learner!

<u>Smart Is Self-Taught</u>

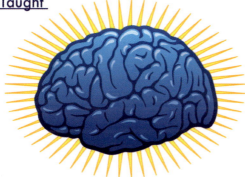

Naming

Big Idea: Learning involves paying special attention to differences.

- Set your purpose and plan for note taking.

- Leave "tracks of your thinking" as you read:
  ★ Use sticky notes, bookmarks or write in the margin
  ★ Use logo-graphics (symbols, or codes as short cuts)
  ★ Look for Signal Words
  ★ Use word parts to help your comprehension

- Create *SmartNotes*
  (Remember - use your own words, symbols, acronyms, abbreviations, bullets, page numbers, etc. to represent your thoughts/ideas.)

  ★ Topic and Date
  ★ Notes Column – add important events, ideas, people, definitions, formulas, etc.
  ★ Cue Words – 3 or more most important words or phrases to go with what you have written
  ★ Include illustrations, doodles, logo-graphics and other visuals to deepen and cement your understanding.

Previewing

Big Idea: Set the stage for self-directed learning.

- Tour the chapter to get a birds-eye view of what you're going to learn and the layout of the context.

- Notice highlights and important features:

Print	Graphic	Visual
Titles	Charts	Pictures
HEADINGS	Graphs	Photographs
Bold print	Lists	Drawings
Italics	Time lines	Illustrations
Colored print	Maps	Sketches
Bullets	Tables	Cartoons
Side bars	Diagrams	Paintings

- Skim the opening and last sentence/paragraph of each section.

Make your thoughts visual by completing the following templates:
  ★ Preview Template
  ★ Getting the Gist
  ★ Word Wall

Connecting

Big Idea: Learning involves looking for how things fit together.

Connect background knowledge with new knowledge!

Choose from the following graphic organizers to help you see similarities, chunk information into categories, and organize your learning in the visual ways:

- **Mind Maps**
- **Attribute Web** – (to describe the topic)
- **Similarities Connector**
- **Differences Connector**
- **Flow Charts** – (for step-by-step procedures and operations)
- **TimeLines** – (for key dates, order of events or happenings)

Project Guide: Create Your Own StudyWhiz System

Recapping

Big Idea: Meaningful learning happens in stages.

Thinking about your thinking!

Before moving forward, stop and check your progress! Ask yourself: How well do I understand this material? Do I know the information well enough to move into new material?

Use the following Recapping templates:
- 80-20 Rule (prioritize: most and least important ideas)
- Know Chart (make your present study status visible)
- Recap Rubric

Constructing

Big Idea: Taking learning beyond the textbook to make it your own.

Use it, or lose it!

Using information from your other MindFrames, create *StudyBriefs* to improve your memory and understanding, study for tests, write essays, complete projects, give speeches, and shine during class discussions!

Choose from four different kinds of StudyBriefs:
- **Terms/Concepts** (for key ideas, important concepts, terms, points of emphasis)
- **People** (for learning about people in history and scientific advancement, plus characters in literature)
- **Events** (for action in stories, historical events, and significant occurrences in science, mathematics, and technology)
- **Other** (something that doesn't seem to fit)

Self-Testing

Big Idea: Self-testing helps fears before a test — and makes you proud after the test!

Rehearsing!

- You can use all your MindFrames to make tests and reviews for yourself and peers.
- Arrange your **StudyBriefs** in an order that makes sense to you and helps you remember information.
- Make an updated **Know Chart**
- Create Talking Points to tell a story of what you've learned.
- Tell your story out-loud to build memory power.
- Check your understanding with a **Self-Test Rubric**.

Reflecting

Big Idea: Reflecting puts things in perspective. It leaves you changed!

Reflection begins with "you." In order for learning to leave "you" changed, you need to think beyond yourself and ask, What does this information mean to:
- my family?
- my friends and peers?
- my community?
- my country?
- humankind?

Create a learning journal by recording your reflections:

Content Journal
To record what you found interesting and important in the material you learned and make a general summary.

Personal Journal
To reflect on what this learning experience was like in terms of your feelings, reactions, and insights.

Blackline Masters contained on a CD may be purchased for $6 from:

TriEd Associates, LLC
P.O. Box 1336
Grayson, GA 30017

Please send check or money order along with the address to where the CD should be sent. Thank you.

Made in the USA
Charleston, SC
23 July 2010